Shared Musical Lives

Shared Musical Lives

Philosophy, Disability, and the Power of Sonification

LICIA CARLSON

OXFORD
UNIVERSITY PRESS

Oxford University Press is a department of the University of Oxford. It furthers
the University's objective of excellence in research, scholarship, and education
by publishing worldwide. Oxford is a registered trade mark of Oxford University
Press in the UK and certain other countries.

Published in the United States of America by Oxford University Press
198 Madison Avenue, New York, NY 10016, United States of America.

© Oxford University Press 2022

All rights reserved. No part of this publication may be reproduced, stored in
a retrieval system, or transmitted, in any form or by any means, without the
prior permission in writing of Oxford University Press, or as expressly permitted
by law, by license, or under terms agreed with the appropriate reproduction
rights organization. Inquiries concerning reproduction outside the scope of the
above should be sent to the Rights Department, Oxford University Press, at the
address above.

You must not circulate this work in any other form
and you must impose this same condition on any acquirer.

Library of Congress Control Number: 2022909750

ISBN 978-0-19-761835-6

DOI: 10.1093/oso/9780197618356.001.0001

1 3 5 7 9 8 6 4 2

Printed by Integrated Books International, United States of America

*To my J's
and to all who find a voice in music*

Music: breathing of statues. Possibly:
stillness in pictures. Speech where speech
ends. Time upright and poised
upon the coastline of our passions.
—Rainer Maria Rilke, "To Music"*

* William Gass, *Reading Rilke: Reflections on the Problems of Translation* (New York: Basic Books, 1999), 38.

Contents

A Pandemic Preface   ix

    Sonification: An Overture   1

1. A Brief Taxonomy of Musical Others   13
2. Musical Selves   19
3. The Epistemic Force of Musical Encounters   36
4. Wordlessness Is Not Worldlessness: A Lyrical Interlude   54
5. The "Musical We"   60

    Conclusion: Musical Worlds   77

    Coda: A Remarkable Serendipity   81

Acknowledgments   83
Notes   87
References   107
Index   115

A Pandemic Preface

When I began work on this book a number of years ago, I could not have envisioned our present moment. As I write this, we are experiencing a pandemic on a global scale and incredibly painful upheavals in the United States in response to the violence and oppression that are part of the deeply entrenched racism in American society. Both of these circumstances have only deepened my sense of the importance of music as a means of expression, human connection, and change.

The diverse modes of shared music that have flourished during the pandemic are powerful and profoundly moving. During widespread lockdowns, musicians found ways of sharing their art with others, from online recordings and livestreaming concerts to playing music from balconies and rooftops and serenading healthcare workers as an expression of thanks and solidarity. Despite the many forms of isolation that this pandemic has engendered, social connections have been transposed into musical ones. Music as a healing force, live and recorded, has been mobilized in hospitals, outside residential facilities such as nursing homes and assisted living centers, and in virtual memorial services. Professional musicians have shared their talents with the world, while friends and family members have found ways to make music in the intimacy of their homes, both in person and virtually.

The political force of music also reverberates amid the ongoing protests for racial justice in the United States. Though composed a number of years ago, the songs in *Seven Last Words of the Unarmed* by composer Joel Thompson give musical expression to the tortured last words of the victims of police violence.[1] The principal clarinetist for the New York Philharmonic, Anthony McGill, inspired hundreds of musicians (including myself and some of my colleagues at the Longwood Symphony Orchestra) to "take two knees" (#taketwoknees) as a form of musical protest.[2] And musicians around the world played musical tributes and held violin vigils to protest the murder of Elijah McClain, a twenty-three-year-old whose death underscores the lethal intersection of race and disability in this profoundly unequal and discriminatory system.[3]

The power of music has been deeply felt during these moments of suffering, uncertainty, and unrest. And yet sadly, the instances and impacts of discrimination against disabled people, or ableism, have also intensified. This pandemic has exposed the disproportionate, often lethal burden on disabled persons: structural impediments to accessing necessary care and treatment for Covid-19 and other conditions, rationing protocols and justifications for refusing care to people with disabilities (including people with intellectual disabilities) based on erroneous assumptions about their diminished quality of life and moral worth, the tragic number of deaths in residential care facilities, and forms of isolation and marginalization that compound existing vulnerabilities and forms of oppression.[4]

The twin focal points of this book—that musical encounters can be a source of knowledge and are ethically significant, and that disabled lives have value and ableism in all its forms must be challenged—have taken on a new shape and urgency in the current moment. It is my sincere hope that these philosophical reflections will confirm the importance of music as a means of deepening our human understanding and show how shared musical experience can contribute to the creation of a more hospitable world.

Sonification

An Overture

As an undergraduate, I volunteered at the Rehabilitation School in Poughkeepsie, New York, in a classroom with children who had a range of disabilities. Though I never brought in my violin to play with them, many of our encounters were musical ones, as we listened to music together, danced, conducted in the air, and moved along to the rhythms and harmonies. I still remember a boy named Scott, who would ask for the classic '80s song "Big Country" and would be absolutely beside himself with excitement each time we listened to it. Lisa, who didn't speak verbally, would conduct along with music of all genres and then grab my hands to dance. I began to wonder what philosophers had to say about disability, and what I found bore no resemblance to the students with whom I spent a few hours each week. The gap between these rich musical lives and the characterizations I found in philosophy sparked a desire to explain this disconnect and to answer the question: Why is intellectual disability the "philosopher's nightmare."[1]

I am fortunate to play in the Longwood Symphony, a community orchestra made up of mostly medical professionals whose mission is to share "the healing art of music." This experience has shown me that the intersections of music, medicine, and disability can be found far beyond the clinical setting. In 2015, we had the privilege of playing with the internationally renowned pianist Nobu Tsujii, who performed Beethoven's Piano Concerto No. 5. Having been a part of many chamber and orchestral ensembles over the past four decades, I have always been fascinated by the phenomenological aspects of musical performance. How is it that we communicate as musicians with one another, with soloists, and with conductors? How do we experience our bodies and the music, both individually and collectively? What are the forms of connection that allow us to blend sounds, to breathe and move together, to become the music as both one and many? The experience of performing with Tsujii, who is blind, generated new questions and recast old ones. What expectations and assumptions about *disability did the orchestra members, conductor, and audience bring to the performance? What role did Tsujii's disability play in this musical encounter, and how did it shape the experience for all involved?*[2]

In 2016, I attended an interdisciplinary conference on music and cognition where I was introduced to the practice of sonification and learned of a fascinating application of this technology.[3] *In the most general terms, sonification is "the use of non-speech audio to convey information."*[4] *In one presentation, researchers were using sonification to translate EEG data from epileptic seizures into musical sound with a dual aim: to increase accuracy at identifying seizures by training clinicians to "hear" them and to eventually find ways for patients to manage, predict, and perhaps ultimately control their seizures.*[5] *This technology raises interesting questions about the nature of perception and the value of music in clinical contexts. Why is it easier to hear these episodes rather than see them on the EEG? What does this suggest, more broadly, about the nature of musical cognition and perception? What revelatory power can music have in other contexts?*

This book is not a musical or philosophical autobiography,[6] but I begin with these three examples of how music, philosophy, and disability have intersected in my life as a way of giving some context for what motivated me to write about them together. Though I double-majored in music and philosophy in college, I kept my musical and philosophical lives separate for many years. As I pursued research on philosophy and intellectual disability, music was always there as a trusted friend, a source of joy and comfort, of reprieve and rejuvenation, but it did not figure into my philosophical work. Yet the musical encounters I had as an undergraduate remained with me, and I eventually decided to return to them and to bring music into the fold.

Dissonances

My experience with the students at the Rehabilitation School and the research that it prompted revealed a stark dissonance to me. As I began to wonder whether any philosophers (past or present) had anything to say about people like Scott and Lisa, I was shocked to find that the "severely cognitively disabled" were often discussed in connection to nonhuman animals, with questions about their personhood (usually *whether* they were persons) dominating these arguments. There was a profound dissonance between the often attenuated depictions of people with intellectual disabilities in moral philosophy and the complex lived realities experienced by these individuals and those close to them. My book *The Faces of Intellectual Disability: Philosophical Reflections* was an attempt to make sense of this jarring contradiction by critiquing elements of these dehumanizing "faces" as they appear in both the historical and philosophical worlds of intellectual disability. The exploration of the *musical* faces of intellectual disability in the chapters that follow here can be read as another response to this dissonance.

When I turned to work in the philosophy of music, however, a second dissonance emerged: a tension between the richness and vivacity of musical experience and the limits of philosophical discourse to give voice to this lived, embodied dimension of musical performance and engagement. Philosopher Kathleen Higgins articulates this tension in her call to move beyond traditional philosophical treatments of music: "Western aesthetics has become skeptical of the easy connection that most of the world makes between music and ethical life. In particular, the field's tendency to treat music as an autonomous structural object and to minimize concern with the holistic character of musical experience (which depends significantly on context) has obscured the experiential bases for recognizing music's symbolic and motivational roles with respect to ethical living."[7] Rather than focusing on the nature and status of the autonomous "musical work" or making judgments about the quality or aesthetic value of particular forms of music, this book builds upon calls like Higgins's to expand philosophical approaches to musical experience.

In looking to see what philosophers had to say about music and disability together, I found a third dissonance between the significant attention paid to music and intellectual disability in many other fields (including psychology, music therapy, music education, special education, and disability studies) and the silence of philosophers on this topic. The paucity of philosophical discussions of disability in relation to musical experience and the arts more generally was in stark contrast to the myriad connections and burgeoning work on music and intellectual disability in these other disciplines. This is not necessarily surprising, given that much of the focus on intellectual disability in philosophy has been centered primarily on ethical and bioethical questions of personhood, rights, definitions of quality of life, and treating disability as a marginal case or as a problem to be solved.[8] In moving the philosophical conversation into the realm of the arts and musical experience, I hope to challenge and recast many of these ethical questions and offer different portraits of intellectual disability and flourishing. My work has been profoundly shaped by the interdisciplinary field of disability studies, where there is already ample work focused not only on music but on theater, visual arts, and aesthetics more broadly.[9] The richness of this literature and the cultural vibrancy of disability arts should serve as an invitation to philosophers to join these conversations and broaden our philosophical horizons when addressing disability.

Sonification

After being introduced to the concept of sonification at the NEMCOG conference, I was intrigued and decided to look into it further. I discovered that this technology, which has been around for decades, has widespread application, not only in scientific and technical settings but also in the arts. Sonification can be defined as "the use of non-speech audio to convey information. More specifically, sonification is the transformation of data relations into perceived relations in an acoustic signal for the purposes of facilitating communication or interpretation."[10] The field is quickly expanding across disciplines, and one can find researchers sonifying data as varied as DNA, particle physics, seismological data (an early example of sonification was the Geiger counter), and physiological information such as heart rate, skin temperature, and blood pressure.[11] Moving into the arts, some composers are using sonified data as a basis for musical compositions, such as the fascinating "Listening to the Mind Listening" project, and thus crossing and blurring the boundaries between art and science.[12] There are also some interesting connections between sonification, music, and disability. Wanda Diaz Merced, an astronomer who lost her sight in her twenties, has used sonification to convert astrophysical data into audible sounds. As an intern at NASA, she developed "a prototype data analysis tool that would familiarize blind people with space-physics data. So we developed software that could map astronomical data into sound—its pitch, rhythm and volume."[13] Not only has sonification allowed her to continue her research, but it has also yielded important discoveries. Merced stresses that the value of this technology extends beyond scientists with visual impairments: "because astronomers usually separate out different frequency components into many graphs, [the fluctuation of electromagnetic emissions] is easy to miss. With sonification, we can listen to all the different frequencies together and pick out the signal from the noise."[14]

This concrete example of using audible tones to express something in different terms, thereby enhancing comprehension, resonates with my own views about the value of musical experience to have this kind of revelatory power in the context of both philosophy and disability. Therefore, I will extend the concept of sonification beyond its technical uses and transpose it into a philosophical key to serve as the organizing principle for the ideas in this book. For my purposes, I will speak about sonification on two levels. First, *sonification* is the process by which musical experience reveals dimensions of the self and transforms our relationships to others; second, on a more theoretical level, *philosophical sonification* refers to the analysis of these concrete forms of sonification and the knowledge they yield and involves a critical (re-)examination of philosophical concepts, arguments, and theories with a musical attunement.

There is another reason I find the idea and practice of sonification compelling. In bringing science, technology, medicine, philosophy, and the arts into dialogue, it is premised on the notion that there is value to be gained from these forms of cross-pollination. This mirrors my own conviction that expanding philosophies of disability to include the arts and to critically engage with work in fields beyond the humanities is not only valuable but essential in working toward disability justice.

The two central arguments of this book are grounded in this commitment. First, in the same way that one may be able to better interpret an EEG that has been translated into audible tones, I will argue that musical experience can *sonify* important aspects of ourselves and our relationships. Insofar as *shared* musical experience can generate particular forms of knowledge about oneself and others, it is epistemically valuable; and given the ways in which music can establish, transform, and enable certain forms of human connection, it is ethically important. Versions of these two claims have been made by people as diverse as philosophers of music, poets, novelists, musicians, musicologists, composers, neuroscientists, physicians, music educators, and music therapists. What is distinctive about my approach, however, is that I make a philosophical case for the relevance of musical experience, for its powers of sonification, in the context of disability.

Why bring philosophy, music, and disability together under this new conceptual umbrella? Shared musical experience can call forth and reveal certain dimensions of the self, expand the moral horizon on which ethical questions are posed and answered, and reconfigure modes of being in the world with others. Thus, attending to musical experience has the power to challenge problematic assumptions about disabled people and the concept of disability itself and can trace new paths for philosophies of disability.

Definitions

Before I begin, I want to briefly clarify my use of the two central concepts at the core of this project: music and disability. In speaking about *music* and musical experience, I have in mind what Christopher Small has called "musicking": "to take part, in any capacity, in a musical performance, whether by performing, by listening, by rehearsing or practicing, by providing material for performance (what is called composing), or by dancing."[15] I am interested in music in the broadest sense of the term, and the arguments I make are not restricted to particular musical genres or settings (e.g., Western classical, instrumental music, professional musicians). This is not to say that differences in musical forms, styles, or modes of production are unimportant, nor do I want to suggest that the context within which music is experienced is irrelevant. In focusing on the concrete, lived, embodied musical experience, I want to keep the scope of consideration as broad as possible at the outset, so as to include a vast range of musical experiences.

Disability is an equally difficult term to define. It is a heterogeneous, often contested term that has been defined in multiple fields (medicine, psychology, the law, genetics, and education, to name a few) and by a range of experts, professionals, disability activists and advocates, and disability theorists. The categories of "intellectual and developmental disability" and "cognitive disability" are no less varied and are equally historically and conceptually complex. The disability rights movement, which emerged alongside other civil rights movements in the 1960s and '70s, came on the heels of parental advocacy movements in earlier decades; it redefined and continues to shape the meaning of *disability*. In response to the "medical model" and "personal tragedy models" of disability that view disability as an individual pathology that is objectively undesirable and in need of fixing, rehabilitation, or cure, disability rights activists and theorists have proposed models of disability that locate the problem in the "misfit" between bodily/mental differences and the social and structural environments in which they are lived.[16] As the interdisciplinary field of disability studies has burgeoned over the past three decades, increasing attention has been paid to the meaning and significance of disability as a political and social identity, a material embodied experience, a shared community with a distinct history and culture, and a source of disability pride. The field of critical disability studies has opened up even more expansive theoretical and political spaces within which to examine structural forms of oppression, emphasizing the importance of postcolonial work on disability and the complex intersections between disability and other identities.[17]

It is within this critical disability framework that I situate my own discussion of intellectual and cognitive disability. While I will refer to specific terms and classifications in the chapters that follow, I use "intellectual disability" broadly to refer to conditions and "impairments" that affect cognitive and intellectual function, development, and behavior and that fall under this umbrella term in professional discourse.[18] However, I recognize that "intellectual disability" is a complex category with a specific historical and philosophical lineage, and I employ it without assuming that it is a self-evident, unproblematic "natural kind." That said, I have chosen to use the term here because the individuals who bear these labels have distinct experiences and, in some cases, musical lives that have been overlooked and are important to acknowledge. There are also debates surrounding "person first" language; some people prefer to use the phrase "person with a disability," whereas others prefer "disabled person." Unless otherwise specified in a particular case, I will use both interchangeably to denote individuals who self-identify and/or have been defined by others as having an intellectual and/or developmental disability. I do this as an acknowledgment of the diversity of preferences within the disabled community.

At times, I use "cognitive disability" to refer to a broader category that includes intellectual and developmental disabilities but also conditions that affect cognition such as dementia, Alzheimer's disease, and traumatic brain injuries. I will also include the perspectives of people who have been diagnosed with autism (autism spectrum disorder) and/or self-identify as autistic and/or on the autism spectrum. This, too, is a contested category, and there are individuals who prefer to speak about neurodiversity rather than employ and endorse clinical classifications. It is also important to note that some autistic people also have intellectual or developmental disabilities, while others do not. Finally, in some instances, I refer to designations of severity such as "profound" and "mild." Though I recognize that these are somewhat artificial designations and I do not view them as absolute or unproblematic, they do capture certain constellations of capacities that are relevant to my discussion.

Parallels between Music and Disability

In bringing music and disability together in these philosophical reflections, I have been struck by a number of parallels between them. First, music and disability are central parts of the human experience. This is not to suggest that music is an important part of everyone's life or that all individuals will experience disability. But the possibility of becoming disabled is shared by everyone; Rosemarie Garland Thomson has argued, "What we call disability is perhaps the essential characteristic of being human."[19] Concepts, practices, and attitudes regarding disability structure our communities and our social and political lives in distinct ways, and as many people with disabilities have pointed out, even those who do not have a disability are "temporarily able-bodied." Similarly, the experience of music, in its variety of forms, is ubiquitous. Though it may not have *universal* reach, for so many individuals and cultures, musicking is woven into the fabric of their everyday lives. Second, there is an embodied, performative dimension to the experience of both music and disability. Neither the lived experience of music nor that of disability is static, and the dynamism of both will be explored in the chapters that follow.

Finally, as I discussed above, music and disability present complex definitional challenges that raise important questions. The "musical work" and the "disabled body" or "disabled mind" bear the marks of institutional, disciplinary, technological, scientific, and social structures and conventions that remain contested and the source of much debate. Their meanings are embedded in historical and material contexts. As work in both feminist philosophy of music[20] and feminist disability theory has underscored, it is impossible to consider the experience of music or that of disability in a vacuum; they intersect not just with gender but with race, ethnicity, class, and sexuality.[21] Music and disability, as both concepts and lived experiences, are shaped by social and cultural norms and material conditions and have been defined by a variety of "experts" in a range of professional disciplines. While this point may seem obvious or unnecessary to make, it is important given the tendency by some to essentialize both "music" and "disability," a move that I want to resist in both cases.[22]

I want to conclude this section with a few clarifications about my approach. Disability is often present in academic conversations in ways that perpetuate, rather than move beyond, harmful stereotypes and erroneous assumptions. People with intellectual disabilities have been represented and treated as the *other*, as medical curiosities, freaks, or inspirational heroes, as tragic victims, recipients of pity, passive patients who are in need of fixing, or individuals who are incapable of leading meaningful lives. In a musical context, this might mean an exclusive focus on the musical savant, the nonverbal exotic other, or the divine mouthpiece.[23] In exploring the intersection of music and intellectual disability, it is not my intention to engage in or encourage these forms of "othering" or enfreakment; rather, I hope to challenge and move beyond them. At the same time, I also want to avoid universalizing claims about the significance of music for disabled people. Musicking is always defined and determined by particular material, structural, and uniquely individual conditions. In arguing that the musical lives of people with intellectual disabilities can provide a counterpoint to certain erroneous and dehumanizing assumptions, I do not intend to argue that the capacity for musical expression, engagement, or enjoyment is in any way a *necessary* feature that an individual must possess to have their dignity and humanity respected or a requirement for rich interpersonal relationships.

Moreover, though I will argue that there can be tremendous ethical and epistemic value to musical encounters, music can also cause harm, undermine human relationships, and be weaponized to work *against* justice and well-being at both the individual and collective level.[24]

In this respect, neither my treatment of music nor that of intellectual disability should be read as overly aspirational. I am aware of a dual danger here, that in celebrating the musical lives of the intellectually disabled and music's ability to capture the deepest dimensions of our existence, both are reduced to the mysterious. This, in turn, risks treating them both as "exceptional," where only the intellectually disabled are somehow *truly* able to access music in all of its mystery, and music is considered the *only* art that can bring people together. I flatly reject both of these arguments.

I also resist couching my arguments in therapeutic terms. The vast and varied field of music therapy has much to say about music and disability, and it provides valuable resources, methods, and practices that can benefit people with cognitive and intellectual disabilities. However, rather than focusing on the *rehabilitative* or *normalizing* function of music, I want to move the discussion of music and disability away from a medical and therapeutic context. This is not to say that music cannot serve these aims. But in recognizing and exploring the meaning, richness, and possibilities of shared *musical lives* in a more inclusive and expansive way, I want to make room for voices and experiences that fall outside the purview of music therapy and that have been ignored, discounted, or marginalized in philosophy.

The final point I wish to make here is about the scope of this project. The inspiration for this book stems from an interest in what music can reveal about the experience of disability, and vice versa, and why this is philosophically significant. By bringing music, philosophy, and disability together, many of the arguments in this book bear directly upon disability and intellectual disability in particular. Yet I also address broader questions about music, identity, and ethics that are not restricted to the experience of disability. This book is intended to open a philosophical space that includes a broad range of music and musical experiences, including performing, listening, witnessing, and composing. So while intellectual disability is a central leitmotif that recurs throughout, it is not the exclusive focus of these reflections. Because the arguments I am making may resonate beyond the boundaries of both disability and philosophy, they are an invitation to all readers to reflect on how musical encounters can shape and sonify aspects of our lives and our relationships to others.

Overview of Chapters

The book begins with a brief taxonomy of "others," both human and nonhuman, that one encounters through music.[25] These include performers, listeners (or witnesses), and composers, as well as instruments and the musical work itself. While the subsequent chapters explore the relationships with and between performers and witnesses in far greater depth, chapter 1 spends some time addressing the significance of our connections to musical instruments, the ontological status of the musical work, and the presence and absence of the composer when we experience these musical works.

Moving from the "other" to the "self," chapter 2 examines how musical experience for composers, performers, and musical witnesses contributes to the sonification of the self in three ways: through self-knowledge, self-expression, and restoring the self. Musical experience contributes to self-knowledge insofar as it can generate insights about the embodied, temporal dimensions of ourselves, our capacity to be moved, and, at an existential level, a sense of both security and the precariousness of our existence. Musical engagement can also serve as a form of self-expression and communication, tapping into the performative dimensions of ourselves and our identities.

Finally, there are a number of ways in which musical experience can be restorative: it can be a means of calling forth the self that has receded; it can offer forms of comfort and what Tia DeNora calls "musical asylum";[26] and it can give voice to forms of oppression and suffering. The second part of the chapter examines the ways both music and disability are performative and explores these forms of sonification of the self in relation to the musical lives of people with intellectual disabilities.

Chapter 3, "The Epistemic Force of Musical Encounters," considers what it might mean for music to have moral force and yield particular forms of knowledge. In "Musical Morality," philosopher of music Peter Kivy asks whether music can have moral force in any of the following ways: cognitive or epistemic (it imparts moral knowledge of some kind); behavioral (it can make people behave in a moral way); or character-building (it can make someone a "better human being" in some sense).[27] While Kivy concludes that the absolute musical work (a purely instrumental piece of music) does *not* have moral force, I move away from a discussion of the musical work per se and argue that shared musical experience *can* have cognitive moral force as it allows for the sonification of both sameness and difference.

In the context of disability, attention to and engagement with the musical lives of people with intellectual disabilities can be especially significant, as these musical encounters can facilitate the recognition of a fellow human being and reveal certain capacities, modes of expression, and forms of being that might otherwise go unnoticed. This knowledge is morally salient for a number of reasons: it challenges certain dehumanizing assumptions about individuals with profound intellectual disabilities; it can overcome epistemic barriers in relationships with these individuals; and the knowledge that shared musical experiences generate can be relevant for philosophers of intellectual disability. I also consider certain potential dangers in speaking about music as "humanizing" and in addressing "the intellectually disabled" in ways that may further stigmatize them. I conclude with some epistemological questions regarding how, why, and by whom knowledge through musical encounters is produced.

Chapter 4 offers "A Lyrical Interlude" that draws connections between the *wordlessness* of music and the experience of intellectual disability. Through a series of brief philosophical meditations in dialogue with other philosophers who have addressed the limits of language and the philosophical significance of music, I explore the idea that music has the power to create sonic worlds that are beyond language, that *wordlessness* is not *worldlessness*.[28]

Chapter 5, "The 'Musical We,'" moves into a more in-depth examination of the *shared* dimensions of musical encounters. In the context of intellectual disability, I argue that musical encounters have the potential to change the configuration of relationships, lessen the effects of stigma, enlarge the moral imagination, and transform moral boundaries. Taking Alfred Schutz's concept of the "musical we" as a starting point,[29] I focus specifically on what it means to share musical time, spaces, and joy with others; how shared musical experience can transform and transpose relationships; and the nature and significance of musical presence. These forms of connection are particularly ethically significant in establishing and expanding relationships with and between individuals with intellectual disabilities. The chapter ends with an examination of four specific virtues that can be cultivated both within and beyond the musical encounter: empathy, acknowledged dependence, humility, and solidarity.

The conclusion, titled "Musical Worlds," considers how the arguments in the book have laid the foundation for a number of interdisciplinary counterpoints and harmonies that can be generative for future work in the philosophy of disability, philosophy of music, and disability studies. It offers some final reflections on the meaning of musical worlds and the transformative power of musicking.

1
A Brief Taxonomy of Musical Others

Experiencing music involves coming into contact with a multiplicity of others. Yet who and what are these others? In what ways do they shape my engagement with music and populate the musical worlds I enter? Many of these questions regarding musical encounters with otherness are prompted and shaped by my own experiences playing the violin in many different settings and musical ensembles. In this chapter, I offer a brief taxonomy of some of these others as a way to paint the musical landscape against which the subsequent chapters will emerge. Some of these others are fellow human beings with whom I share particular musical moments, some are voices from the past, and still others are objects (both solid and ineffable) that shape and define musical experience. While some will figure more prominently in the larger arc of this book, they all play a role in various forms of sonification that establish the "musical we."

Insofar as music is most often an intersubjective art, we encounter many different others that demand our attention and call upon us to recognize and respond to them in distinct ways. Our musical worlds are populated by many other persons: composers, performers, and listeners or beholders of music.[1] Depending on the circumstances, these others may be proximate or distant, living or deceased. In some instances, I share the role with them if we are co-performers or fellow audience members; in others, they are less immediate. Yet they all play an important part of my musical life, and as the later chapters will consider, they help to define and shape the "musical we." There also are inanimate others I encounter in musicking: the score, the musical work itself, recordings, instruments. Each of these musical others poses distinct and interesting philosophical questions. Though my focus in the subsequent chapters is primarily on human musical subjects, I would like to elaborate a bit here about musical instruments and the musical work, as they are equally important elements in the musical encounter.

Objects have an independent existence of their own, yet they also become part of our lives in intentional and often unexpected ways. With musical instruments, the musician is in a sense both the master of the object and entirely dependent on it. As I reflect on the relationship I have with my violin, I recognize that the instrument becomes a part of me, it is a way that I am able to communicate, and my voice emerges from it. It cannot speak words, but together we produce gestures, rhythms, and meaning. Through my movements, I give it a voice, yet its sonority, timbre, and resonance are also its own. I both find and lose myself in the process of fusing with the violin; we become a single expressive unit, and yet at the same time, as I encounter technical challenges and strive to produce the desired sound, I am constantly reminded that this object is also *not me*. Chilean poet Pablo Neruda captures the richness of our shared lives with objects in his "Ode to Things." These final lines of the poem speak to the relationship one can have with objects, and I would add to his list a musical instrument:

> O irrevocable
> river
> of things:
> no one can say
> that I loved
> only
> fish,
> or the plants of the jungle and the field,
> that I loved
> only
> those things that leap and climb, desire, and survive.
> It's not true:
> many things conspired
> to tell me the whole story.
> Not only did they touch me,
> or my hand touched them:
> they were
> so close
> that they were a part
> of my being,
> they were so alive with me
> that they lived half my life
> and will die half my death.[2]

A second other that raises more complex questions regarding its existence is what many refer to as "the musical work." There has been ample discussion within the philosophy of music about the nature of the musical work itself. First, it is important to recognize that the term is a historically contingent, regulative concept that emerged in the nineteenth century.[3] Even while recognizing the historical context in which one encounters the musical work, however, its existence raises intriguing ontological questions. Phenomenologist Roman Ingarden, in his *Ontology of the Work of Art*, argues that the musical work exceeds any concrete limits placed upon it and cannot be reducible to the score, the intentions of the composer, the mental experience of the listener, or any particular performance of the work. Ultimately, he argues that it encompasses a heterogeneity of qualities and says that though we engage with it intentionally, "it remains something that is transcendent to all concrete individual mental experiences."[4]

Bruce Benson argues that Ingarden's account and the very language of "the musical work" are both problematic because they fail to recognize the performative dimension of music. Thus, he prefers to speak about the musical "piece": "On the one hand, as long as we think of pieces of music as being 'works' with ideal existence, we are inclined to overlook or else downplay the role of performance."[5] In fact, Ingarden does acknowledge the significance of musical performances; however, he distinguishes between the philosophical task of recognizing the musical work as an intentional object in all of its complexity and the experience one has with a particular performance, what he calls our "everyday commerce" with it: "the process of this commerce occasions a wholly different conception of the musical work, namely, that according to which it is an object enduring in historical time that slowly, yet inevitably, changes."[6] Yet how does this everyday commerce with the musical work constitute a distinct experience, and what are the elements of this musical encounter?

My experience of the musical work is temporal and embodied. Yet if we consider various musical subjects (composer, performer, and beholder), each has a distinctive relationship to the musical work. As a performer, my engagement with the music is more direct and immediate in two respects. First, I become the physical vehicle through which the work is concretized, whether through my voice or through the instrument that becomes an extension of myself. Second, in order to perform a work, I possess a degree of knowledge about the piece; the work, both my part in it and the piece as a whole, is present for me both physically and cognitively in a way that it need not be for those witnessing it. While the audience member's mind may wander or she may not be fully engaged throughout the piece, the musician must remain deliberately present in order to continue to perform the task at hand. As the performer, then, I enter into this musical work in all of its dimensions—its rhythm, melody, harmony—in ways that I do not as a listener or spectator. As the witness of a musical performance, while I *may* be brought into the sonorous and visual world of the piece I am experiencing cognitively, emotionally, and physically, I am not giving voice to it myself. My relationship to it might be compared to the viewing of a painting or a sculpture, whereas the performer of a musical work is simultaneously enacting the musical work, bringing it into existence once again. Mikel Dufrenne captures this difference: "For us, musical sound is simply perceived. But for the artist, it must first of all be produced. The artist enacts a dialectic of the perceived and the produced, of the spontaneous and the formalized."[7] The performer, then, has a distinct relationship to the piece, as it is her responsibility to give voice to the piece, a process that involves freedom and creativity, as well as a certain fidelity to the composer's intentions.[8]

The musical work is dynamic by virtue of the fact that it comes into being with each performance in a new setting, with new voices, players, and conductors, offering new tempos, interpretations, and renditions. To recognize this is to acknowledge that musical pieces are capable of transformation, of becoming. And this requires a shift in attention from the work to the performance. As Benson explains, "as long as we think of pieces of music as being 'works' with ideal existence, we are inclined to overlook or else downplay the role of the performance. . . . [T]he identity of a piece of music can only be grasped *as it unfolds and continues to unfold.* The identity of a piece of music comes at the end, not at the beginning. Since pieces of music are never static, their identity—like any other thing that is alive and growing—is one that never reaches a point of complete definition."[9] This performative, generative, dynamic aspect of the piece suggests that it can be viewed as a process of becoming rather than a fixed entity. Even if one recognizes the fixity of the notes in the score, the prescribed sequence of tones, harmonies, melodies, and rhythm (i.e., the musical elements that make a piece distinctly what it is), every performance leaves room for improvisation and interpretation, and no two performances are identical.

Yet the musical work itself may also generate encounters with other kinds of others contained within it. If there is accompanying text, then the narrative that is presented can open up a field within which I encounter real or fictional characters, storylines, actions, and emotions. In the context of disability, Joseph Straus explores the way in which musical modernism fosters the occasion for an encounter with disability in multiple forms and registers. This can be both positive and negative, stigmatizing and liberatory: "the modernist musical response to disability is complicated, abounding in ambivalence, conflict, and self-contradiction. . . . But even amid a eugenic culture and a tendency toward the exoticization and enfreakment of disabled bodies, modernist musical representations of disability often open up new perspectives on disability. They reveal the aesthetic and physical beauty of disability, and change our sense of the beautiful in the process."[10] In examining a range of modernist musical representations of disability (including aspects of "idiocy," "autism," and "madness," among others), Straus shows how the musical work itself can have transformative potential by fostering encounters with forms of otherness in unique ways.

Any discussion of the musical work must include a discussion of its creator, the composer. And while defining the composer does not raise the same ontological challenges that the musical work presents, the presence and absence of the composer and the relationship the composer has with both performers and audience members are worthy of attention. In one obvious sense, every encounter with a musical work that is deliberately produced by someone else is an encounter with the composer. Alfred Schutz characterizes this relationship between composer and musical subjects (be they beholders, performers, or readers of the score) as follows: "Although separated by hundreds of years, the latter participates with quasi simultaneity in the former's stream of consciousness by performing with him step by step the ongoing articulation of his musical thought."[11] Yet the performers and the audience do not encounter the composer in precisely the same way; they do not retrace the composer's steps through the same means. The performer's experience of the music is arguably more immediate and intimately connected to the composer, as the performer is responsible for bringing the composer's creation to life again. The composer's presence is integral as I follow the musical instructions, pass over the musical paths forged by the composer, and reiterate the notes, harmonies, melodies, and dynamics given to me.

Yet there is also a way in which the composer may recede or be absent for both the performer and the witnesses of the composition. First, it is possible to experience a piece of music without knowing who composed it. While knowing who the composer is *may* affect my perception of it, this is not necessary for me to engage with a musical work and be moved by it.

(Of course, the degree to which I fully *understand* it in all its musical and technical nuances is a separate issue that would clearly be affected by my knowledge of the composer's identity.) It is interesting in this context to consider what Michel Foucault has called the "author function." In addressing what is at stake in attaching an author to a literary text, Foucault asks what role knowing the author plays; does anonymity add to or detract from the experience, and why are we so wedded to knowing the author? We can ask a similar question of the musical work and its composer. While knowing the composer can provide important context and direction for performing and receiving a musical work, might anonymity have a freeing effect, permitting even greater interpretive possibilities for performer and audience, and thus shape the musical encounter in new and unexpected ways? We might ask of the musical work and the composer function what Foucault asks of the literary work: "What difference does it make who is speaking?"[12]

As the subsequent chapters will confirm, it *does* matter who is speaking musically, through the many voices and modalities that musical experience affords to composers, performers, and witnesses alike. In the pages that follow, these human musical subjects (more than the musical work itself and the instruments) will feature most prominently, with a particular focus on how people with intellectual disabilities can occupy these various roles. It is to these musical subjects that I now turn.

2
Musical Selves

How can engagement with music and multiple forms of musical experience yield knowledge about oneself? In what ways does music shape identity and allow for self-expression? In speaking about the value of music, philosopher of music Jerrold Levinson describes music's "self-affirmation value": "Musical works arguably help to crystallize or constitute the self that attends to them, internalizes them, and identifies with them."[1] The ways in which this might occur are, of course, varied and complex. In her philosophical investigation of these aspects of musical experience, Kathleen Higgins identifies multiple ways that music can serve as a vehicle of self-knowledge, an area that has been neglected by many philosophers of music: "We encounter music as engaged and embodied *selves*. Music's impact on self-conception is rarely considered. . . . Many facets of the experience of human selfhood become apparent through music."[2] For Higgins, these include our existence as temporal beings, our vulnerability, and our capacity for joy.

This chapter will explore how musical experience (for composers, performers, and musical witnesses alike) contributes to the sonification of the self in three distinct ways: through self-knowledge, self-expression, and restoring the self.[3] Musical experience contributes to self-knowledge insofar as it can generate insights about the embodied, temporal dimensions of ourselves, our capacity to be moved, and, at an existential level, a sense of both security and the precariousness of our existence. Musical engagement can also serve as a form of self-expression and communication, tapping into the performative dimensions of ourselves and our identities.[4] Finally, there are a number of ways in which musical experience can be restorative: it can be a means of calling forth the self that has receded; it can offer forms of comfort and what Tia DeNora calls "music asylum"; and it can give voice to forms of oppression and suffering.

Music and Self-Knowledge

The dynamic nature of musical experience means that individuals engaged in this activity are inhabiting a particular space, place, and mode of being. But in what ways am I aware of myself during this experience? First, all musical experience is embodied. Whether I am listening to a piece of music live or recorded, playing an instrument or singing alone or in concert with others, or composing or improvising my own musical work, I am doing so as an embodied being.[5]

As a performer (whether in a formal or informal setting), I am aware of myself through the movement of my body, its connection to the instrument, and the ways in which, through my movements and gestures, I *become* musical. When I perform a piece of music, I become aware of my own physical existence, with all its possibilities and limitations. The ways in which the instrument becomes a part of me (or, in the case of the voice, *is already* a part of me) allows me to perform an aspect of myself that may otherwise lie dormant, awaiting expression. There is also a cognitive dimension to my performance, whether I am playing someone else's composition or my own. The musical act is at once physical, emotional, and cognitive and requires a unique combination of these three elements, all of which may in turn become objects of my self-reflection. In enacting a musical performance (be it solitary or in concert with others, for myself alone or with an audience), I experience my movements, my flexibility and inflexibility, my mastery and effort, and my limitations. Though I am distinct from the various others identified in chapter 1, I am also fused with them in certain significant ways. When I perform, the instrument becomes an extension of my body, a part of myself. In *The Sonic Self*, Naomi Cummings describes the performer's experience of embodiment as follows:

> I know myself as somebody, an acting *body*. I know how an action on the violin "feels." I know "what it is like" to experience my body as a sounding medium in a social space.... The self-reflexivity developed by a performing musician has to be such that she can take an awareness of herself as a sounding body in an acoustic space.... In the process of changing my relationship to space, I discover a new possibility of "self," a new construction of my embodied position.... No one can know "what it is like" to experience my particular body, working with my particular violin, in this particular space, unless I give my own first-person report.[6]

Cummings suggests that each individual's embodied experience of music is unique, and I would add that there is a distinctness to each musical moment as well. Thus, my changing relationship to space and to my embodied position is not static, depending on the kind of musical performance or encounter I experience. If I am performing my own composition or improvisation, I direct my body to move accordingly, and the performance becomes an embodied expression of myself. If I am not performing my own musical work, I inhabit the musical world created by the composer, and my bodily gestures and actions are not only self-directed but also guided by the demands of the music that has been given to me. If I am playing in an ensemble or performing for an audience, my sense of space and embodiment is shaped by their presence as well.

Yet musical experience is not only embodied for the performer; through the experience of witnessing music, we experience our own bodies as dynamic, responsive, and engaged. Though so much of our experience of music today is via recordings and virtual, even in these musical encounters, the body is present. As contemporary jazz pianist and composer Vijay Iyer, who has written about music, cognition, and embodiment as both a performer and a researcher, observes: "More than a century after the invention of recording technology, we have become accustomed to recorded, disembodied, electronically generated music. But still, music tends to bear these same traces of embodiment."[7] Iyer argues that music tells stories and, in doing so, "explodes narratives" through the performer's embodied presence: "Kinesthetics, performativity, personal sound, temporality—all these traces of embodiment generate, reflect, refract stories into innumerable splinters and shards."[8] In becoming a part of these musical narratives, not only through the perception of musical sound but in the movements that one may make along with the rhythms and percussive vibrations of a musical performance, the musical witness experiences and can recognize dimensions of her own embodied existence.

In addition to calling attention to my existence as an embodied being, musicking also reveals my complex relationship to time. This is because music itself is a temporal art. In "What Is a Temporal Art?" Jerrold Levinson and Philip Alperson explain: "Objects of [temporal arts like music] generate a kind of time that is peculiar to them, that exists for a perceiver only in and through experience of the work."[9] In the words of Susan Langer, "Music makes time audible, and its form and continuity sensible."[10] As Langer's words capture so eloquently, music facilitates the sonification of time itself;

through music, time *becomes sound*. Music unfolds in time, and thus both performers and musical witnesses enter into musical time and can experience their own temporal existence in distinct ways that intersect and diverge.

But how might this musical time be understood?[11] In phenomenological terms, Edmund Husserl discusses the perception of a melodic line as a way of exploring our apprehension of temporal objects. We do not experience melody as a chain of discrete and independent tones; rather, because we are able to anticipate and remember certain notes, we perceive them as a whole and continuous temporal object.[12] Music necessarily involves movement and rhythm, and so it unfolds according to its own temporal structure. In this way, it draws me into a specific kind of inner, musical time that can be distinguished from ordinary time. Alfred Schutz defines a piece of music as "a meaningful arrangement of tones in inner time." This inner, musical time is "meaningful to both the composer and the beholder, because and in so far as it evokes in the stream of consciousness participating in it an interplay of recollections, retentions, protentions, and anticipation which interrelate the successive elements."[13] Listening to the slow and fast movements of a Beethoven sonata, for example, can change the beholder's perception of time, move beyond ordinary time, and place one in a new temporal horizon: "While listening he lives in a dimension of time incomparable with that which can be subdivided into homogeneous parts. The outer time is measurable; there are pieces of equal length; there are minutes and hours.... There is no such yardstick for the dimension of inner time the listener lives in."[14] Even within the piece, and within particular measures, a performer can play with the length of particular notes and seemingly elongate or constrict the passage of time without changing the overall tempo.[15]

As a performer, I must enter into the appropriate musical time in ways that shape my perception of my own temporal being. As a musical witness, I may also enter into this musical time, though in ways that are distinct from those of the performer. The audience can be swept up in the rhythm and motion of a musical piece or phrase, thus "keeping time" in a way similar to the performer. Yet there are differences: while the performer is required to dwell within the music's temporal demands, the audience can join or exit this musical time at will. Moreover, my experience of time when present for a particular performance may vary depending on myriad factors: the context or space in which I experience the particular work, my familiarity with the piece itself, the moment in which I am attending the performance, and the influence of other performers and the conductor. The degree to which I "lose myself" in the performance can also shift the perception of the passage of time: I may feel as if I have been transported away to a musical world where, if I am swept up in a piece, time may seem to fly by quickly or slow down. My perception of time can also accelerate or slow *within* the confines of a particular piece, depending on both musical and extramusical factors.

All of these features of musical experience suggest that music shapes our perception of ourselves as temporal beings, consciously during those musical moments as well as in ways that go undetected until one reflects upon the experience after the fact.[16] Yet there are other dimensions of temporality associated with music. In addition to the ways in which our experience of chronological time either maps onto or is distinct from musical time, we can also leave musical traces of ourselves and in this way preserve ourselves as beings who dwell in both the past and the future. In *Music and Ethical Responsibility*, Jeff Warren explains, "Music is not autonomous. Composing, performing and listening to music are not separate from other activities in the world. Music is always linked with human beings, because in creative and experiential acts we leave traces. The 'trace' shows that all musical experience is connected to people and their acts."[17] Whether it is through a recording of a particular performance, in the memory of a shared musical performance or event (on the part of any of the parties present), or in the form of the lasting score of one's composition, remnants of our musical selves remain. Bruce Benson says that "all performance is resuscitation."[18] Musical selves, too, can be resuscitated insofar as our musical lives and experiences may exist beyond ourselves. For the composer and the musician, musical performances provide a way of ensuring a kind of permanence for the self. Insofar as the score outlasts the composer, music is a guarantee of overcoming our corporeal finitude. By virtue of recordings, the same can be true for performers as well, as the sonic worlds they have created are repeatable long after they have been created.

Musical experience also engages our sense of the future. In this respect, it can provide a sense of what Higgins has called "existential security": "Music encourages a sense of safety within the world. . . . Music conveys the possibility of things continuing well, a possibility that is important to us as intentional beings who project ourselves into the future."[19] Insofar as musical perception involves perception of sequences, she goes on to say, "The tensions and resolutions, as well as the general sense of motion conveyed by music, all depend on our awareness that musical events are organized sequentially in time yet perceived as connected."[20] Though musical experience can afford a sense of security in that we anticipate a stable and predictable future and resolution, this may not always be the case. There are instances of music being used for creating terror or fear (which I will address more fully later), and there are also ways in which music can be deliberately created to disrupt a sense of security and stability.

Because musical experience is temporal, it can also affirm our vulnerability and finitude. The fact that any musical performance occurs in a determinate amount of time, that melodies disappear in an instant, reminds me of my own fragility and finite nature. Like the musical piece, I, too, will come to an end. Of course, there are musical works specifically written on this theme of mortality or to honor the dead. But the contingency of all music, and the ways in which traces of the musical work remain even though the particular performance vanishes in time when it is finished, mirrors the trajectory of our own finite yet meaningful human lives.[21]

Musical experience also calls upon us to attend to the past and recognize it as both part of us and yet not fully determining us. In discussing the various ethical dimensions of jazz improvisation, Garry Hagberg identifies "rethinking the past" as central: "One's relations to one's own past, to one's aspirations for the future, and to others... are never fixed. And the moral responsibility to tell and retell, to continuously interweave, is born of that fact.... Jazz improvisation, within the special world of responsive, attentive, creative, and interactive ensemble is itself an example of the ever-changing lived realities of our interactions with others, our interactions with our own pasts, and our creative engagement with our own and others' life-narratives."[22]

In addition to revealing aspects of our embodied, temporal nature, musicking can yield distinct forms of self-knowledge through the sonification of emotions[23] and can reveal what Higgins calls one's "vulnerability to being moved."[24] Depending on the nature of the experience, its context, and my role in it, I may experience musical joy differently depending on whether I am performer, composer, or witness. Each form of musical joy may be in a distinct key, each with its own unique rhythm, harmonies, and timbre.

Musicking in all forms can provide the occasion to experience and gain insight into multiple dimensions of our lived, temporal, embodied selves. I am not suggesting that music alone affords us these forms of self-knowledge; however, insofar as musical experience can draw forth and bring to our attention certain aspects of our embodiment, our cognition and emotions, and the temporal dimensions of ourselves, music performs this distinct task of *sonification* of the self that is worthy of attention. As I will argue in subsequent chapters, these features of musicking will turn out to have both epistemic and ethical significance when we consider our relationships with other musical subjects and the meaning and value of shared musical experience.

Musical Expression and Communication

The activity of musicking involves various modes of communication and expression. And depending on what roles one occupies (composer, performer, witness), musical experience can be both creative and generative. For the composer, music can be a way of expressing emotions and ideas and creating a soundscape allowing both witness and performer to partake in this sonic world. There is a debate within the philosophy of music as to whether a musical phrase or piece (particularly "absolute," purely instrumental, music) has semantic content and if it does have meaning, what the nature of that meaning is. Though I do not intend to engage in this debate here, I do believe that any musical composition, be it through sound alone (either absolute or programmatic music), or through the combination of music and text, can be experienced as a mode of human expression. And the sonification of the self through the creation of musical narratives can be especially powerful: autobiographical narratives, articulations of personal and political struggles, heartbreak and romantic adventures, individual and collective histories, and assertions of identity across genres can serve as a means of both individual and group expression.[25]

While the composer's use of music as a vehicle for self-expression may be considered the most obvious, performers also sonify the self through music. If the performer is also the composer, there is no distinction between the two, while in other cases, the composer–performer lines may be blurred. In jazz improvisation, for example, individuals can be both "resuscitating" particular musical pieces or melodies and at the same time giving voice to new musical ideas and forms. If the performer is distinct from the composer, the musician embodies and expresses the composer's ideas while inflecting them with her own expressive gestures and ideas,[26] thus engaging in a kind of mimetic activity that also generates a unique performance bearing the mark of the performer's own identity. The performer–witness boundary is also blurred because, unless it is a solo performance, the musician must also be a witness of her fellow performers. She is listening, likely even more attentively than the audience; her modes of expression inevitably depend on and are realized through her fellow musicians' musicking as well, and thus these separate performances become one. In this way, in musical ensembles, there is an expression of both the individual and the collective body that simultaneously inheres in and transcends the self.

One might ask what the musical audiences or beholders of music could possibly contribute to the generative process of creating and performing oneself through music if they are simply passive spectators. Yet, as Iyer reminds us, for the musical spectator or listener, there is an embodied, dynamic dimension in which the witnesses themselves become part of the musical world and contribute to this unique, generative event. Whether witnessing a musical performance in a formal or informal setting, live or recorded, I may express myself in any number of ways: through bodily movement and through my responsiveness to particular musicians' actions or musical ideas. In fact, part of what adds to the uniquely creative and dynamic dimension of any musical performance is the collective experience of also witnessing the rest of the audience enacting and reacting to musical moments.[27] Of course, social conventions and expectations can also shape and dictate the nature of these musical encounters, and depending on the genre of musical performance, one may find oneself in very different surroundings (e.g., the concert hall vs. the rock concert).

Another dimension of self-expression for musical witnesses can be found in the very choice of music one makes. One's musical taste and musical sharing can be modes of crafting and presenting oneself to others. In experiencing and expressing emotion in response to a particular piece of music, I am simultaneously performing a dimension of myself that others can witness and that can have a profound effect on them as well.

Music as Restorative

A third dimension of the sonification of the self through musical experience is the restorative dimension of music. Perhaps the most common association with this idea is through the use of music as therapy. Yet, rather than speak about music in this specialized, professionalized context exclusively, I want to consider broader aspects of musical experience that can be restorative and, thus, transformative. First, musical experience can serve to call forth a self that may otherwise have receded or be undetected through more conventional means. Second, musicking can create a world that provides a respite from other dimensions of one's existence and can be the basis for care and what Tia DeNora calls "music asylum."[28] And third, musicking can give voice to certain forms of oppression and suffering in ways that can be significant and transformative for performers, witnesses, and composers alike.

Musical experience not only yields self-knowledge and expression, but it also can call forth a self and enable a return to oneself. In speaking about improvisation, French existentialist and musician Gabriel Marcel writes, "I have found improvisation more than just a refuge. It was an incomparable mode of interior self-repossession.... While for me improvisation has functioned perfectly as a way of recollecting myself, it has done so ... by means of a grace of which I cannot give an account, by restoring to me through the sacrament of sound all those who have shared in my life."[29] What might Marcel mean by "self-repossession" here? It may depend on whether one is a musical witness, composer, or performer. There are ways in which playing music, even in less formal settings, can allow for one to recapture oneself through the narrowly focused activity of producing music (whether alone or with others). One must be entirely self-aware, in terms of both one's embodied movements and one's mental attention, and this may allow for other aspects of the world to recede as a musical self comes into focus.

There is also ample evidence of the effect music can have on individuals with dementia, brain injuries, or cognitive disabilities, where through being in the presence of music or performing music, the self (re-)emerges.[30] In his book *Musicophilia*, Oliver Sacks presents numerous cases of patients who, through music, are able to recover aspects of themselves that had disappeared. The notion of re-calling a self that has receded raises a deeper question about the relationship between music, identity, and memory. To what extent is it appropriate to speak about the *recovery* of a diminished or lost self, and to what degree may it be more fitting to speak about a new/distinct self insofar as musicking allows for new modalities of being and identity to emerge? Yet Sacks suggests that the emotional responsiveness that he witnessed in his patients with dementia need not be tied to memory: "The perception of music and the emotions it can stir is not solely dependent on memory, and music does not have to be familiar to exert its emotional power. I have seen deeply demented patients weep or shiver as they listen to music they have never heard before.... Once one has seen such responses, one knows that there is still a self to be called upon, even if music, and only music, can do the calling."[31]

Another dimension of music's restorative power is to offer comfort and a respite from other dimensions of existence. In her rich exploration of the multiple meanings of "asylum" in *Music Asylums: Wellbeing through Music in Everyday Life*, DeNora traces connections between the medicalized, restrictive spaces of institutional asylums and the power of musical experience in a broad range of settings to enhance flourishing and, in doing so, to offer alternative forms of asylum: "I describe how music, as a specific form of cultural activity, can be practiced in ways that offer what I shall speak of as 'asylum.' I use the term 'asylum' to denote respite from distress and a place and time in which it is possible to flourish."[32] The musical asylums that DeNora explores are not relegated to a medicalized conception of music therapy, however. These can be spaces of rest and repair for the self, whereby musical experiences can bring one back to oneself, a return perhaps to a former self, and offer succor and the possibility of flourishing for a future self.

A third form of restoration that musical expression offers is to give voice to forms of oppression and suffering in ways that have ameliorative and empowering effects. This is something that is evident in many varieties of music, and there are countless examples, both past and present.[33] In some instances, music has offered a reprieve from truly horrific forms of imprisonment, bondage, and subjugation. The songs sung in slavery, the political and subversive forms of the blues sung by women who embodied early black feminist ideas, and the subsequent complex and rich development of the African American musical tradition all reveal musicking as an expression of history, of agency, and of the cry of suffering.[34] In the words of Cornel West, "The form and content of Louis Armstrong's 'Alabama' and Sarah Vaughan's 'Send in the Clowns' are a few of the peaks of the black cultural iceberg—towering examples of soul-making and spiritual wrestling that crystallize the most powerful interpretations of the human condition in black life. This is why the best of the black musical tradition in the twentieth century is the most profound and poignant body of artistic works in our time."[35] As West's description indicates, these forms of musical recovery and restoration happen not only on the individual level but also on the collective scale. Work songs, hymns, anthems, and other forms of musical expression give voice to the possibility of collective healing and restoration as well as individual asylum.[36]

There is, of course, no question that music can serve to organize, intensify, and perpetuate forms of suffering as well. One has only to think of the horrific use of music in the Nazi camps and as forms of torture or "sonic warfare," both past and present. Though in such situations of extremity, musicking can sometimes serve as a mode of resistance, relief, survival, and even transcendence, it is vital not to assume that there is something *intrinsically* or *necessarily* "beneficial and morally good" in all musical encounters.[37] For this reason, it is all the more important to consider under what conditions musicking *can* provide the kind of benefit and "asylum" that we are considering here.

The restorative power of music can be understood as a kind of sonification of the self, insofar as musicking can serve as a means of self-expression, comfort, and empowerment in the face of suffering. It can also be a means of recovery for dimensions of the self that have vanished or diminished. The few examples I have mentioned here have only grazed the surface of the depth and significance that musical experience can have. And expanding the consideration of these performative, transformative, and restorative dimensions of musical experience to include disability further deepens and complicates these modes of sonification.

Performing Music and Disability

If musical experience can generate forms of awareness and self-knowledge and allow dimensions of the self to emerge and to be restored, what might this mean in the context of disability?[38] First, both disability and music are performative. While it is obvious that music is inherently performative, disability is equally performative in complex and significant ways. In their book, *Bodies in Commotion*, disability theorists Carrie Sandahl and Philip Auslander state: "[T]o think of disability not as a physical condition but as a way of interacting with a world that is frequently inhospitable is to think of disability in performative terms—as something one *does* rather than something one *is*."[39] Drawing from Joseph Straus's book *Extraordinary Measures*, Blake Howe explains this in a musical context: "the disabled performer has a 'dual task: to perform music and to perform disability.' The cultural scripts associated with both performances shape each other, so that it becomes difficult or even impossible to disentangle them."[40] Stefan Honisch has described the affirmative dimensions of his own experience as a disabled pianist who uses a wheelchair: "physical difference itself can become the site of the wholly contemporary project of testing boundaries and challenging entrenched conventions, thereby enabling the individual and collective re-thinking of the nature of limitations, ability, and potential."[41] In this sense, then, musical performance intertwined with the experience of disability becomes generative rather than limiting; it can be productive and celebratory rather than merely compensatory or falling prey to what some disability scholars have called the "overcoming" narrative, whereby music is viewed as a means of overcoming one's disability. Honisch and Howe are both speaking about performers with physical disabilities in formalized performance spaces. In considering the role that disability plays in musical performance, Howe emphasizes the way in which disability is constructed *through the musical performance* based on a number of factors. He writes that "with sufficient accommodation . . . stigmas attached to bodily difference may be neutralized, even reversed. . . . Such is the constructed nature of disability that some performance impairments are accommodated while others are not. . . . Like the blurry distinctions between inability and disability, . . . accepted musical accommodations and forbidden musical accommodations lie along a continuum; their rigid separation is entirely artificial and culturally determined."[42] This is a good example of the ways in which the experience and perceptions of disability and "disabled bodies/minds" are context-dependent in musicking, both for the disabled person and for those with whom that person is engaged.

Given the plethora and range of disabled performers, it is impossible to generalize about how disability figures into their experience of music and the identities that musicking generates. But in scenarios where disability is an integral part of the musical performance, this can give rise to new forms of "sonic identity." What Howe calls "disablist" music is "a musical practice that rejects the normal performance body and instead molds its performance practices around the impairments of its performers. Rather than concealing or silencing a disability, disablist music audibilizes disability, asserts disability, even claims disability as a fundamental component of its sonic identity."[43] The British Paraorchestra, for example, includes "talented disabled and non-disabled musicians playing old and new repertoire, that includes digital or assistive instruments alongside traditional ones. . . . This new 'breed' of orchestra belongs at rock festivals just as much as in a concert hall, reaching the broadest range of audiences."[44] The expansion beyond the confines of traditional classical music has significant implications for the intersection of disability and music. In *Music, Disability, and Society*, Alex Lubet argues that jazz is in many ways more hospitable to musicians with physical disabilities than the Western classical world: "the protocols of jazz provide better opportunities for musicians with disabilities not only to perform, but to perform in ways that are actually expressions of lives with disabilities."[45] But even within more traditional classical genres, disabled artists are finding ways of performing and sonifying elements of themselves, whereby their disabilities inform and shape the performance and the nature of the work itself. Molly Joyce, an innovative composer and performer whose relationship to her music and instruments is intimately bound with her disability, states, "Disability informs my practice in that it compels me to produce work only a disabled body can produce; work that can't be compared to standard notions of ability. . . . As a composer and performer largely working in the classical music tradition, which involves instruments that have been around for centuries for very specific bodies of specific abilities, disability from a social model perspective frees me from conforming to such instruments and tradition. It allows me to consider the lived experience first and foremost and then find the resulting musical material."[46] Scottish percussionist Evelyn Glennie suggests that though her deafness shapes her perception and the ways she engages in her craft, she does not categorize it as "disabled music": "I don't categorize the music I play—it is simply a painted aural sensation that can be experienced or felt as a physical medium or simply heard through the ears should the listener choose to. Each person, deaf or hearing with all its variations, has the capability to experience the performance in more diverse ways than they think should they allow their minds to open up to those possibilities."[47]

These examples have focused on physical disabilities, but what about individuals with mental, cognitive, intellectual, and/or developmental disabilities, individuals who do not identify as "neurotypical"? In some cases, while musical performances are not *erasing* the fact of disability, they allow musicking to become the central focus. The Me2 Orchestra, the world's only orchestra for "people with mental illness and people who support them," was founded by Ronald Braunstein, whose own professional career as a conductor was halted for a number of years because of his bipolar disorder. As Braunstein and many of the members of the orchestra emphasize, the experience of playing music and performing together has created a stigma-free space in which musicking takes center stage, while also acknowledging and respecting the lived realities of its musicians and providing a community of solidarity and friendship.[48]

In their discussion of the Drake Music Project, a London-based program devoted to making music accessible, Michael Watts and Barbara Ridley write about what performances did for musicians with learning disabilities: "Live performance ... allowed them to assert their identities as musicians, and in doing so, challenge the normative perceptions of society that place their dis/abilities ahead of their musicianship. Music making, therefore, was a means of putting their dis/abilities into their proper place and it gave them the opportunity to create and share something to be judged by its own criteria rather than with reference to their dis/abilities."[49] This statement shows the close connection between musical identities and the ways that disabled musicians' music may be received.

In the collection *Music and Autism*, the conversations between ethnomusicologist Michael Bakan and ten different people who identify as being on the autism spectrum reveal a range of perspectives on the significance of musicking and the complex ways in which music *sonifies* the self. Ibby Grace, for example, writes that for her, music is a way to communicate emotions that were otherwise difficult to understand and to express: "I found out when I was in my youth that I could communicate a great deal of emotion in song. ... In music, I could create empathetic communication about things I had heard other people talking about, and feel it through myself, even with no experience."[50]

In addition to enabling disabled people to express and *perform* their identities through music, the fact that many musical compositions are non-linguistic opens up even greater possibilities for some individuals. Both the composition and the performance of music are generative acts that, though wordless, are capable of creating a sonic world in which something is expressed and experienced. For individuals with disabilities who cannot or choose not to express themselves verbally or for whom language cannot fully capture what they wish to express, musicking can become a way of engaging in the world that is fundamental to their sense of self.

Japanese composer Hikari Oe was born with disabilities that prevented him from speaking and became able to express himself through his compositions. His father, Nobel Prize–winning author Kenzaburo Oe, writes, "If Hikari had not composed, he would surely never have been able at any time in his life to convey the rich, profound, crystalline and radiant message contained in this music."[51] Oe's forms of musical expression exemplify how an individual who by other measures may be deemed "abnormal," whose quality of life may be assumed to be minimal, is able to convey the richness of human experience to others.[52] At the same time, it is important to recognize the dangers of obscuring Oe's music by capitalizing solely on the profundity of his disability. As Straus writes, "Oe's story, particularly the story of his disability, have dominated discussions of his music. Most reviewers have found themselves virtually unable to offer an appraisal, or even a detailed characterization of the music, so overwhelmed were they at the nature of his disability. Most accounts follow the familiar trope of the overcoming of disability cast as inspirational tearjerker: the triumph of the human spirit over adversity. The critical reception of Oe's modest musical achievement is entirely engulfed by the stigmatic trait of his disability."[53] Rather, Straus advocates engaging with disabled musicians in a "realistic mode" that resists these stigmatizing tropes and filters.

Though one might claim that there is something unique (or at least very rare) in Oe's talents as a composer, other forms of musical experience by individuals who have intellectual disabilities but are not considered "savants" can be equally powerful, as we shall see in the next chapters. For individuals with Williams syndrome, for example, music is often a central feature of their lives, one that profoundly shapes their sense of self. In his chapter "A Hypermusical Species: Williams Syndrome," Sacks recounts numerous examples of the ways in which people with Williams syndrome display a "panoply of musical talents."[54] Much has been written about the connections between Williams syndrome and musical ability and experience,[55] though it again is important to resist approaches and framing of their musical lives in ways that further exoticize them.

In cases of individuals with intellectual disabilities that are considered severe or profound, certain dimensions of selfhood may emerge through music, from distinct cognitive capacities, expressions of self-awareness, and preferences to the capacity to experience and share in musical joy. John Vorhaus and Adam Ockelford offer a number of vignettes that illustrate this narrative, performative potential of music in relation to the self.[56] They argue that these examples reveal how "engaging with music, at all levels, can promote a sense of self in children and young people with learning difficulties, and how such engagement can serve as a proxy indicator of self-awareness and identity, particularly in those who are incapable of linguistic communication."[57] Here we see instances of individuals whose modes of self-expression and being in the world would be restricted if bound to verbal modes of communication. However, when placed in the context of musicking, the self is sonified in distinct ways.[58] In this sense, we can also speak about music as transformative, whereby new forms of emotion, expression, and well-being are enabled. The musical joy that Higgins speaks of can differ depending on whether one is a performer or a witness. And in some cases, it may contribute to the performance of a self for whom flourishing may have been assumed to be out of reach.

Another dimension of the sonification of the self that I discussed earlier is the way musical experience structures and refashions one's experience of time and space. These musically inflected temporal and spatial dimensions of existence can be particularly significant for people with intellectual disabilities as well. First, the possibilities of entering into musical time as either musical witnesses or performers present an alternative to the ways chronological time can structure and further disable and disadvantage individuals with intellectual disabilities. If one considers the past designation of intellectual disability as "mental *retardation*,"[59] it conveys the notion of one who is slowed, out of step with "normal" developmental time. Children and adults who fall under this classification system are measured on a developmental, temporal scale that experts use to draw a distinction between chronological and mental age. In fact, one might argue that the very distinction between these two "ages" signals the intolerance we have for such dissonance. Yet, in musical worlds with their own temporality, these designations may no longer be relevant or meaningful.

Second, within the realm of the musical, the possibilities for movement in time are radically different. Unlike normalized, structural temporal demands and constraints that determine the pace of activities and that often define one as falling outside the boundaries of normalcy, musical experiences generate and move to a rhythm and tempo of their own. Dancing, movement, and performance can all alter and even erase these normalized expectations and, in liberating one from them, provide new occasions for "keeping" time, being "in or on time," and reveling in new rhythms and tempos.

We encounter others not just in musical time but in musical spaces as well. In some cases (e.g., the performance hall), there are conventions, normative rules, and particular structures that govern who can enter these spaces and how they must behave. In many cases, these are not, in fact, accessible to certain individuals for a broad range of reasons (physical barriers, behavioral expectations, economic costs, "unruly bodies"). To borrow a phrase from Foucault, we expect "docile bodies" in the concert hall. Yet musical spaces are created and filled far beyond the concert hall and can provide the basis for shared experiences that might not otherwise occur between certain individuals.

Some spaces and forms of music asylum can provide new venues for cultivating musical lives and selves. One example can be found in New York City. After Daniel Trush survived significant brain injuries, his family established Daniel's Music Foundation, a space that offers free music lessons, ensembles, and concerts for individuals with physical and developmental disabilities. Their website states: "Our longstanding goal is to use the power of music to create opportunities for acceptance and respect while enriching the lives of individuals both within the community we serve, and the greater community at large."[60] What is striking is that this is not a therapeutic space with the goal of curing or of restoring "typical" function; rather, it is an open space of creativity, musical joy, and community. Daniel's father remarked that the prospect of one more therapist appointment, which would have been one-on-one with a music therapist, was not the musical experience he envisioned, and this was in part what inspired the creation of the foundation.[61]

Musicking in a broad range of settings has the ability to offer alternative forms of asylum and a means of flourishing. DeNora defines this power as "the ability to feel as if one is in the flow of things, to be able to feel creative and to engage in creative play, to enjoy a sense of validation or connection to others, to feel pleasure, perhaps to note the absence, or temporary abatement, of pain."[62] This constitutes a distinct kind of musical flourishing. Spaces of musical asylum that allow musical selves to emerge need not only be sought in medicalized, clinical spaces or in formal performance settings. For many people with intellectual disabilities, who may be marginalized and assumed to have limited modes of self-expression, enabling musical encounters can be profoundly transformative, allowing them to cultivate and perform their identities in rich and varied ways.

Thus far, I have focused on modes of sonification of the self. But how are these dimensions of our musical selves, and the roles that musical experience can play in performing, restoring, and transforming the self, relevant when considering the *intersubjectivity* of musical experience? How does shared musical experience yield new forms of knowledge about fellow musical subjects? How can it create new spaces, worlds, and modes of being with others, and change the ethical configurations of relationships? And why is attention to intellectual disability in the context of musicking philosophically important? Chapter 3 will begin to address these questions.

3
The Epistemic Force of Musical Encounters

As chapter 2 has illustrated, musical experience can reveal aspects of the embodied self and, in some cases, can call forth a self in ways that are restorative and transformative. These dimensions of musical experience are not restricted to the individual alone; they can have a profound impact on relationships *between* musical subjects. Through musicking, we encounter many different "others" who demand our attention and, in some cases, call upon us to recognize and respond to them in distinct ways. So in what ways might these encounters with musical others, these shared musical experiences, be ethically significant?

The idea that music can have moral force is not new in the philosophical tradition. Dating back to Plato and Aristotle, one can find arguments regarding the power of music to shape moral character and the importance of musical education.[1] Yet the question of whether and *how* music can have this moral force is far from settled. In "Musical Morality," philosopher of music Peter Kivy poses this question, with a focus on instrumental or "absolute" music. In asking whether music can have a moral force, Kivy begins by arguing that if what one means by this is the ability to bring about good in the world, it seems unlikely.[2] But he then goes on to entertain three ways one might say that music has this power. Music has *cognitive* or *epistemic* force if it "conveys or imparts moral insights and theoretical knowledge"; it has *behavioral* force if it possesses the power to make people act in a moral way; and it has *character-building* moral force if it can "make someone, as it were, a better human being, either in the more obvious moral dimensions, or in any other way that might be broadly conceived as part of the moral."[3] Kivy concludes that absolute music does not have moral force in any of these three ways. Rather than taking up his arguments regarding absolute music directly, I would like to shift the focus of the question from absolute musical works to *musical encounters* and consider how shared musical experience may have moral force. In this chapter, I will focus on the first of these, epistemic or cognitive force.

Kivy argues that, unlike the teachings of Aristotle or Kant, for example, absolute music cannot have epistemic force because it is not propositional in the way that philosophical texts are. Moreover, even if absolute music were able to express something distinctive (as some have argued), it is "hardly the stuff to impart epistemic moral force of any significant kind to works of absolute music."[4] Yet if we shift the focus from the musical work itself to shared musical experience, there are ways in which musical encounters *can* yield knowledge that is morally relevant.

While chapter 2 looked at how musicking can sonify the self through modes of expression, communication, and self-knowledge, this chapter will focus on the *epistemic* force of musical encounters and ask, how can shared musical experience yield knowledge not just about myself but about others whom I encounter? In the context of disability, attention to and engagement with the musical lives of people with intellectual disabilities can be especially significant, as these musical encounters can facilitate the recognition of fellow human beings through both sameness and difference and reveal certain dimensions of their lives that might otherwise go unnoticed. This knowledge is morally salient for a number of reasons: it challenges certain dehumanizing assumptions about individuals with profound intellectual disabilities, it can overcome epistemic barriers in relationships with these individuals, and the knowledge that shared musical experiences generate can be relevant and valuable for philosophers of intellectual disability.

The Sonification of Sameness: Recognizing a Fellow Human

Music has been argued by many to possess a *humanizing* effect. But this broad claim begs for clarification and raises many questions. What does it mean to humanize? Who or what is being humanized? The musician herself? The spectator? The relationship between them? Is there reason to resist the language of humanization given the ways in which this concept has been historically used as a tool of exclusion? For the purposes of my discussion here, I want to explore the idea that musical encounters can yield important knowledge about the other. We can talk about these musical experiences as humanizing in that they allow us to recognize and connect with these musical subjects as fellow human beings with whom we share something significant.

Centuries ago, philosopher, composer, and music theorist Jean-Jacques Rousseau wrote the following in his treatise on music and language:

> Painting is closer to nature and music is more dependent on human art. It is evident also that the one is more interesting than the other, precisely because it does more to relate man to man, and always gives us some idea of our kind. Painting is often dead and inanimate. It can carry you to the depths of the desert; but as soon as vocal signs strike your ear, they announce to you a being like yourself. They are, so to speak, the voice of the soul. If you hear them in the wilderness, they tell you you are not there alone. Birds whistle, man alone sings. And one cannot hear singing or a symphony without immediately acknowledging the presence of another intelligent being.[5]

Here Rousseau is pointing to two different ways in which music (in this case, song produced by the human voice) reveals a fellow human being. First, in hearing song, we hear "a being like ourselves," since "man alone sings," suggesting that there is something fundamentally human about the production and perception of musical song.[6] In this respect, Rousseau states that music "does more to relate man to man" than painting does, because of its dynamic nature; it "always gives us some idea of our kind." So a musical encounter can tell us *that* we are in the presence of another human being, whether through song, composition, or witnessing an instrumental performance.[7]

Many contemporary philosophers, musicians, and composers have also pointed to this capacity of music to reveal a fellow human subject. Speaking about the fundamentally intersubjective nature of musical experience, jazz pianist Vijay Iyer claims that the very "capacity for music begins with the capacity to recognize another human being."[8] Kathleen Higgins focuses on the shared experience of listeners:

> the physical engagement that we experience in listening to music is a humanizing influence. . . . Music's appeal to our physical nature gives us a very immediate sense of enjoyably sharing our world with others. This sense of sharing is ethically beneficial in that it makes it difficult to consider others' experience alien to our own. In fact, we feel that others' living experience is in this case actually our own. When this occurs, our concerns cannot really seem to us a purely private matter. We rejoice beyond

ourselves in musical experience. I cannot think of a better basis for ethical concern.[9]

For Higgins, then, the musical encounter is significant insofar as it moves us "beyond ourselves." I recognize this fellow subject as similar to myself, insofar as she, too, partakes in and enjoys this shared musical world.

Jerrold Levinson calls this humanizing force of music its ecumenical power: "Ecumenical power is the ability of music to transcend cultural barriers, to disarm prejudices, to unite people *simply as human beings*, regardless of linguistic, religious, or ethnic affiliation. Of course its power to do this is not unlimited, and may be greater for some genres than others, but it is noticeably greater than that of other artistic manifestations, which often struggle to export themselves outside of their culture."[10] As with Higgins's characterization, here, too, it seems that by engaging purely through the music, one leaves other traces of identity behind and is stripped of "affiliations" that might hamper the ability to relate directly with fellow human beings.

In their discussion of the Weimar workshop, which brought together Arab and Israeli musicians to play in an orchestra for the first time in 1999, Edward Said and Daniel Barenboim speak about the power of this shared performance to transcend political differences. Said explains, "It was remarkable to witness the group, despite the tensions of the first week or ten days, turn themselves into a real orchestra. In my opinion, what you saw had no political overtones at all. One set of identities was superseded by another set."[11] And in Barenboim's words, "What seemed extraordinary to me was how much ignorance there was about the 'other.' . . . They were trying to do something together, something about which they both cared, about which they were both passionate. Well, having achieved that one note, they already can't look at each other in the same way, because they have shared a common experience. And this is what was really, for me, the important thing about the encounter."[12]

These examples speak to the power of music to foster a recognition of *similarity* between self and other, whether through performing together, sharing in the capacity to be moved by music, as Higgins discusses, or, as Rousseau writes, recognizing another of one's "kind" through the musical encounter. Insofar as shared musical experience involves this recognition of fellow musical subjects, the suggestion is that other facets of identity fall away.[13] But how exactly does encountering the other and recognizing her "simply as a human being," as Levinson writes, give this musical experience *epistemic moral force*? The power of this mode of recognition in the face of intellectual disability offers a compelling answer.

There is a long history of dehumanizing people with intellectual disabilities in a variety of ways: concretely, through myriad social, institutional, and structural forms of oppression and violence, and conceptually and theoretically, whether at the hands of professionals and "experts" who have classified them, scientific and social theorists who have deemed them pathological and their lives objectively undesirable, or philosophers who have called their personhood and humanity into question.[14] In view of these forms of dehumanization, the power of shared musical experience to *humanize* is significant. My use of "humanize" here involves twin moves: *recognizing* another individual as a fellow human being, often in the face of dehumanizing assumptions and practices, and *connecting* with other human beings *as musical subjects*. There are a number of ways in which these musical encounters can accomplish this: they can provide a mode of expression to those who may not be able to communicate in traditional ways, they can reveal particular capacities that may otherwise go undetected, and, through various forms of musicking, musical encounters can foster distinct forms of engagement between individuals (with and without disabilities). Though I will focus on these three features of musical encounters here, it goes without saying that there are many other modes of recognition and connection that musicking can foster.

Music can offer a means of expression to those who might have limited forms of communication. In cases of individuals with intellectual disabilities who do not express themselves through verbal communication, certain dimensions of selfhood and capacities for engagement can emerge powerfully through music.[15] And insofar as musical encounters can yield important knowledge that, in turn, affects how these individuals are viewed and treated, this mode of sonification is morally significant. Recall the discussion of Hikari Oe in chapter 2. Oe was able to find a means of self-expression through his musical compositions and performances. As his father explains, Hikari's music is not only significant as a mode of self-expression, but it has also offered insight into his world for others: "For our part, had Hikari not composed, *we would have never realized, nor would we have been able even to imagine, that he possessed this sensibility.* The scope of what we might have gained from this world and understood of it would have been significantly narrowed. I feel we would have missed gaining an insight into some of the most important and humble aspects of the meaning of human life."[16]

The varied ways in which intellectually disabled people engage with music (as composers, performers, and beholders) raise questions about the adequacy of our current models that measure cognitive ability, particularly if those rely significantly on linguistic forms of communication.[17] And whereas for Kivy it is precisely the fact that instrumental music has no language or propositional content that robs it of its cognitive moral force, Levinson suggests that it may be this dimension of music that allows us to recognize the other *as* a fellow human being. Of music's ecumenical power, he writes, "This no doubt owes in part to the abstract, non-verbal nature of music, but perhaps also to its greater capacity to enter into us, to take hold of us, to set our bodies and souls in motion, almost without the participation of our wills."[18] In the context of profound disability and for some individuals who do not communicate through speech, this may be where music's power lies, as it is this feature of music that allows them to engage as active, human subjects.[19]

Musical encounters can also reveal intentional behavior, aesthetic preferences, and the capacity to be moved. In *Giving Voice: Mobile Communication, Disability, and Inequality*, Meryl Alper provides a complex examination of communication technologies (specifically, the Proloquo2Go app for the iPad) that "give voice to the voiceless."[20] Her study provides numerous examples of how, through technology, certain characteristics and capacities are able to be expressed. Though different from my focus on music specifically (given that Proloquo2Go is used to "give voice" in language), there are some interesting connections with musicking.

Alper discusses how, through technology, ten-year-old Beatriz is able to express her musicality and preferences: "David [Beatriz's father] also detailed how, through online games, Beatriz displayed a keen ability to understand musical patterns. She frequently played games ... and would hum along with the accompanying music. David said that Beatriz had the ability to recognize the rhythm, start and end the phrasing at the right time, and anticipate the conclusion of the music. 'That tells me that she *knows* the song. She cannot sing it, but she knows it,' he asserted. The inability to produce embodied oral speech did not preclude Beatriz from having an innate sense of what singing was like."[21]

Another example of how technology and music are able to sonify aspects of the self, including the capacity for empathy, is told by Marisa, the mother of Stephanie, a ten-year-old girl with autism: "Marisa felt that therapists dehumanized her child and others like her. . . . Professionals lost sight of the human part."[22] Yet music became one vehicle through which Stephanie's emotional world came into relief: "Stephanie's world, Marisa commented, was deeply emotional despite not being able to express those feelings in spoken words. . . . 'We start to notice about music. Sometime[s] when she feels sad, she put[s] sad music [on] and she [cries]. When she feels happy, [it] is like the way she say[s], 'I feel happy.' While Stephanie's therapists privileged oral speech, Marisa felt that Stephanie voiced her emotions through the songs she chose to play."[23]

These examples point to the power music has to sonify our emotional lives and to reveal the capacity to share in musical joy. In speaking about his daughter, Sesha, who has profound disabilities, Jeffrey Kittay writes: "To make a special occasion with Sesha is to put on one of her favorites and sit next to her to listen. She is rejoicing to the music, we are visibly rejoicing at her pleasure and our redoubled appreciation of the music as we listen to it through her, and she is elated as she sees her musical pleasure shared and validated by those closest to her, so that she is not alone in these feelings both deeply held and finely wrought."[24]

In *Giving Voice to Profound Disability*, John Vorhaus introduces us to Kate, a twelve-year-old who cannot read, speak, or write, though she understands many words and studies the piano. This portrait of her beautifully captures the sonification of all these human elements: cognitive ability, agency, aesthetic preference, musical joy, and human connection through musical encounters. According to her father, Patrick, "She has perfect pitch—and she lives for music; music is her life and soul; if you took music away from her I don't know what she would do." Her piano teacher of many years, James, says: "I love her musicianship above all else. Kate hears everything in vivid colour. At one point she would cry when listening to, say, a G7 chord. She not only hears accurately but she has a very strong emotional reaction." Vorhaus goes on to say:

> What is striking is not only Kate's musicality but her interaction with others. She and James will sometimes sit close together, Kate holding James's arm, imploring him to follow her, or looking intently into his eyes, signaling how she intends to play her next piece. She anticipates what James is expecting of her; she teases and provokes him; she vocalizes to her father, in dictating that she wants him to clap in the rhythm of the music. . . . Kate is able to maintain intimate relationships and to display the complex, intentional behavior that goes along with that.[25]

While people like Kate may possess a rare combination of abilities and may not be typical of all children with profound disabilities, Vorhaus wants to illustrate "how uneven, unexpected, and complicated the profile of capabilities can be in one and the same person. . . . [S]he is unable to read, utter or comprehend the word 'and' but she knows a G7 chord when she hears one; she cannot participate in political decision-making, but *she can initiate and engage in decisions about whether to play the music of one composer or another*."[26] The significance of this example is not to simply reiterate the problematic trope of exceptional ability amid incapacity and disability. Rather, Kate's musical life underscores why it is important to witness each individual in his or her uniqueness and resist facile generalizations and constructed prototypes of the "profoundly disabled."[27]

To claim that shared musical experience can have epistemic or cognitive force, then, is to recognize that music can *sonify* individual emotions, capabilities, preferences, desires, and modes of being that may not otherwise be apparent. The revelation of this particular facet of a person can, in turn, challenge erroneous assumptions and lead to a better understanding of the individual's experience (both musical and otherwise). This can be true for individuals performing or composing music, as with Kate and Hikari Oe, or individuals who are moved as listeners by particular musical pieces, such as Sesha and Stephanie. As these few examples have shown, musical encounters can yield knowledge about individuals with intellectual disabilities that provides a much fuller portrait of their abilities and their subjective lives. Individuals who may be assumed to lack certain capacities in other contexts can, with the right conditions, emerge as fully engaged musical subjects with whom a shared humanity is recognized.[28] While this may not be surprising to disabled people, their families and friends, advocates, musicians, and professionals in a range of disciplines (including music therapy, music education and special education, music cognition, and the performing arts), philosophers have failed to address music and the arts when speaking about intellectual disabilities. Therefore, expanding the consideration of the musical and artistic lives of people with intellectual disabilities *in philosophy* is imperative.

The ways in which intellectual disability has traditionally been defined and discussed by philosophers have been limited and problematic,[29] and the paucity of philosophical conversations about disability and the arts, and intellectual disability and music in particular, is only further evidence of this. With a *very* few exceptions, this is true of moral philosophers, philosophers of music, and philosophers of disability alike. Bringing musical encounters into philosophical discussions of disability can challenge and reshape existing assumptions and claims about personhood, moral status, and quality of life. And recognizing what these musical lives reveal can move the conversation beyond the medical, personal tragedy, and supercrip/savant models of disability and provide an antidote to dehumanizing arguments.

Musical encounters have the power to uncover important dimensions of fellow musical subjects and, in doing so, reveal a shared humanity. Yet to share a musical experience with another human being does not mean that it is necessarily rooted in a perception of *sameness*. Differences do not always recede or get erased through the activity of musicking; musicking can also expose, exacerbate, and transfigure them. To speak of musical encounters as humanizing only based on what I *share* with my fellow musical subjects raises a number of concerns and critical questions. What does it mean to say that music can "unite people *simply as human beings*"? Does this suggest a recognition of sameness, of identity with the other? What forms of sameness shape the contours of a musical encounter? Does this imply that differences fall away, that they are not relevant to the musical encounter? Does partaking in a shared musical experience *necessarily* translate into a deeper recognition of aspects of this other individual? Do certain conditions need to exist for this to happen?

In claiming sameness, there is a danger of discounting the particularity of the other, of erasing or obscuring important differences, whereby the musical encounter becomes simply a means of seeing oneself in the other. In *The Faces of Intellectual Disability*, I argue that people with intellectual disabilities are often placed in the mirror role, where they serve to simply reflect aspects of the non-disabled to themselves.[30] In a similar vein, musical encounters may run the risk of effacing the other and serve only to confirm certain aspects of oneself.

More pressing, however, is the question of whether it is desirable or even *possible* to leave aspects of one's identity behind in musical encounters. Music is experienced by subjects who are fully embodied with a distinct life narrative and complex identities, and these encounters occur within social and cultural structures rather than in a vacuum. Thus, it seems overly simplistic to claim that somehow music strips us of everything but our "bare humanity." There are countless examples from the history of musicking that reveal the many ways in which race, ethnicity, class, sexuality, and gender have affected the perception and treatment of musicians and the production, performance, and reception of music. And there is a growing body of literature that examines the complex ways in which disability intersects with all of these.[31] Even the few examples of people with disabilities discussed thus far show that, though they are engaged, embodied musical subjects, they are also musicking in their own distinct and unique ways, rather than conforming to some predefined mythical "normal" listener or performer.[32] So, while in one sense these examples illustrate the possibility and value of shared musicking between fellow musical subjects, these encounters do not simply involve acknowledging another individual *just like me*. Music does not erase all difference; it may transform and transfigure it and reveal it in important ways.

If we return to the last line of Rousseau's passage, he states that in experiencing song or symphony, we are not simply in the presence of another human being but in the presence of "an *intelligent being*." This suggests that musical artistic production is reserved for particular individuals.[33] To compose or perform a piece of music obviously requires certain skills and capacities: cognitive and physical abilities, musicality, and more. Recognizing this in another is one way in which differences can surface in myriad forms. For example, I see the performer's virtuosity as distinct from my own abilities or inabilities; I recognize the composer's creativity as different from my own capacities; I witness my fellow performers or audience members as bringing their own stories, histories, and experiences to the interpretation of a piece of music or a musical performance; I realize that what I am hearing, seeing, or witnessing is undeniably unique, unlike my own or any other's musical experience.

Unfortunately, in Rousseau's case, when speaking about the fact that in song "man" recognizes others *of his kind*, this "kind" was reserved for a relatively narrow category of individuals.[34] In his exploration of Rousseau's experience of music and disability, Blake Howe discusses Rousseau's reception of a girls' choir in the Venetian *ospedali*. He writes, "The singers had performed their disabilities in the most concealed of ways—inaudibly and (because of their hidden location) invisibly. Rousseau's experience of their music is unproblematic to him until the performers are revealed, and the shock of aural-visual incongruity prompts an episode of self-reflection: why does disfigured appearance not translate into discordant sound?"[35] Here we observe yet another way in which difference, and in this case disability, shapes and defines the musical encounter: the embodied presence of the performers affects Rousseau's perception of their musical abilities and his own experience of the encounter. Versions of Rousseau's question reverberate today, when people express surprise that disabled people (often in conversations about "savants") are able to perform or display talents *despite* their disabilities.

Rousseau's philosophical treatment of music and the disabled "other" points to the difficulties and complexities of speaking in universal terms about the power of musical encounters to humanize through the recognition of sameness. This example also leads us to ask how musical encounters that involve disability (whether they are with or between disabled performers, composers, witnesses, or musical works themselves) challenge the very idea of encountering sameness through music. While I do not want to discount the possibility that musical encounters *can* be a space in which I recognize what I share with fellow human subjects, the question of difference—the ways in which musical encounters reveal another who is distinct and different from me—must not be left behind.

The Sonification of Difference

There is a long legacy of music performing an *othering* function, both in the context of disability and more broadly. These many ways in which musical encounters exacerbate difference and the strangeness of certain others challenge the notion that musical encounters can be humanizing insofar as they facilitate a recognition of sameness, of shared experience. And there is extensive work on disability and music that demonstrates how musicking can exacerbate, rather than mitigate, the perception of disabled musical subjects as other.[36]

In the context of music and intellectual disability, specifically, the musical savant is perhaps the most common example of this. Joseph Straus, in his history and taxonomy of the many different classifications of "savants" that have held sway in both professional discourse and the cultural imagination, argues: "The enfreakment of savants has enshrined them as a species of *super-crip*, people whose unusual ability in one narrow area has enabled them to transcend their general disability. Savants have thus come to be seen as inspirational figures, whose apparent transcendence of disability makes the relative incapacity of their non-savant peers appear even starker by comparison, even as it is understood to offer compensation to the savants themselves for the depth of their deficiencies."[37] Here the recognition of musical ability does not humanize, does not render people with intellectual disabilities *more human*; rather, by perpetuating the view that they are radically other because they have some exceptional talent that is significant against more global deficits, they remain within the realm of the abnormal and even the pathological. Straus also challenges specific myths about musical savants that reside within these theories: that they have rote, mechanistic memory and hence are more like machines than humans; that they do not "learn" their craft, perpetuating the "myth of the untutored savage"; and that they are "incapable of true creativity," in that they are "understood to perform in a constrained, rigid, repetitive, and echoic way, capable of skilled mimicry, but not of creative innovation."[38] Yet Straus is not suggesting that the musical talents and abilities of these individuals are unimportant or that they should be ignored or dismissed. Rather, he advocates rejecting forms of recognition that exoticize or enfreak the musical lives of people with disabilities: "they are people who, like the rest of us, are good at some things and not so good at others."[39] As Susan Wendell has written in her philosophical examination of disability, "The image of the disabled hero may reduce the 'Otherness' of a few people with disabilities, but because it creates an ideal that most people with disabilities cannot meet, it *increases* the 'Otherness' of the majority of people with disabilities."[40]

In the examples I discussed earlier, though some of the individuals had what may be viewed as notable talents, the significance of their musical lives can be acknowledged without falling prey to problematic social scripts that Straus and other disability theorists challenge. These forms of shared musicking are worthy of attention because they can reveal dimensions of another person in all of their uniqueness and difference, something that is possible in musical encounters between *many* musical subjects (not just those with disabilities).

Straus's critique makes clear that it is not enough simply to point to select examples in the abstract when considering how musical experience can yield knowledge about people with disabilities; we must also ask *how* this knowledge is produced, by and for whom, and from within what framework. How do social scripts, expectations, and ableist assumptions and social structures define its production? For example, what is the difference between recognizing and producing knowledge about the musical subjectivity of individuals with intellectual disabilities in an institutional setting (e.g., via a music therapist), through scientific studies on music and cognition (e.g., where people with disabilities are research subjects), or through popularized cultural examples (e.g., through film biographies)? And how can musical encounters resist dominant models such as the "supercrip" and allow for a more realistic recognition of difference? These questions are particularly important to consider given that many people with intellectual disabilities encounter music with the assistance of others, a point to which I will return at the end of this chapter.

Given that all musical encounters take place within a particular context, claims to some kind of universal transcendence of *all* difference through shared musical experience are problematic. Moreover, it is clear that in many instances, the recognition of difference can serve to further pathologize or enfreak the other. Yet sharing in musical experience *can* be a means to recognize another's particularity and differences in ways that are not reductive and dehumanizing. Perhaps the dichotomy of sameness/difference is too stark or even false; if one recognizes the simultaneous ways in which musical encounters can speak to both sameness and difference in ways that are productive, authentic, and generative, there is no need to choose one over the other.

One possibility is that musical encounters humanize, not by the transcendence or erasure of difference but *through* difference. In his discussion of the legacy of African American music, Cornel West returns repeatedly to the notion that music can reveal something of moral significance that bridges both sameness and difference. West's description of the plight and creativity of Black musical artists is rooted in its particularity, yet at the same time, he also speaks to the universality of the experience of music, insofar as it gives voice to a shared suffering, shared existential struggle in the face of the absurdity of existence that gestures more broadly to the human condition: "[My intellectual lineage] . . . reaches its highest expression in music—as in summit because it is the grand archaeology into and transfiguration of our guttural cry, the great human effort to grasp in time (with the most temporal of the arts) our deepest passions and yearnings as prisoners of time. Profound music leads us—beyond language—to the dark roots of our scream and the celestial heights of our silence."[41] Music calls forth the experience of suffering and of yearning, a human cry that is at once universal and yet profoundly particular to one's individual, social, cultural, and historical location.

A powerful example from the world of disability arts is the music of Krip-Hop Nation. In describing the origins of this musical group and its activism against police brutality, Leroy Moore writes, "For years, I collaborated with other activists and artists fighting police brutality against people with disabilities in the street war and the culture war. For hours I listened to Hip Hop artists with disabilities speak out against brutality against our communities.

By 2006, I was motivated to use my years of activism and love of Hip Hop to create a cultural home for Hip Hop artists with disabilities. This was the beginning of what is now Krip-Hop Nation." In 2012, Krip-Hop Nation released a CD that finally gave disabled artists "their cultural expression on this issue of police brutality."[42]

While Moore's and West's examples sonify a shared experience of suffering, attention to musical lives can also challenge certain erroneous assumptions about suffering and disability. I argue that people with intellectual disabilities often represent the face of suffering based on the ableist assumption that they lead impoverished, attenuated lives.[43] Yet the recognition of the richness of these individuals' musical lives and their capacity for musical joy and flourishing can eclipse the personal tragedy model of disability that so often dominates the philosophical imagination when speaking about intellectual disability.

Higgins, too, recognizes this power of music to reveal sameness through difference. She explains that sharing in music, particularly if one moves beyond one's own cultural repertoire, can overcome cultural divisions and enhance our appreciation for our kinship with others: "Our shared musicality is a real ground for developing a sense of human commonality across cultural boundaries, while the range of music we might encounter encourages appreciation of cultural diversity.... We would do well to make more of music's potential to help us recognize our human kinship, however varied our cultures."[44] Though Higgins's point inevitably raises the question of the degree to which musical encounters are culturally mediated (and her notion of cross-cultural musical kinship may create some skepticism), it is interesting to consider the implications of her claims when thinking about cultural difference in terms of disability. Many disabled artists and disability theorists have pointed to the power of the arts to give voice to *disability culture*, and disability aesthetics broadens the scope to include not only musical works but also the alternative modes of musical performance, embodiment, and expression that disability arts enact. As Tobin Siebers writes, "Disability aesthetics prizes physical and mental difference as a significant value in itself. It does not embrace an aesthetic taste that defines harmony, bodily integrity, and health as standards of beauty. Nor does it support the aversion to disability required by traditional conceptions of human or social perfection."[45]

But how, specifically, can musical encounters reveal differences in ways that do not objectify, enfreak, or dehumanize the other? And what might this mean in the context of intellectual disabilities? If we consider this question from the perspective of listeners, or witnesses of musical performances, there are a number of ways musicking allows for the sonification of difference. Straus defines alternative modes of hearing: "Normal hearing is the way in which normally embodied people make sense of music. I would like to counterpoise this with what I will call 'disablist hearing,' that is the way in which people with disabilities make sense of music."[46] In addition to blind hearing, deaf hearing, and mobility-inflected hearing, Straus identifies what he calls autistic hearing. Straus explores the ways in which certain features of an "autistic cognitive style," which, in other contexts, may be pathologized and deemed undesirable, can transform the ways in which music is experienced and shape "a disablist musical hearing."[47] While Straus stresses that he is not making a universal or essentialist claim about *all* autistic individuals, he views his work as contributing to a counter-narrative that defines autism as a form of neurodiversity rather than as a deficit or pathology. Moreover, he argues, "the goal of the enterprise is not so much about how people with disabilities appear to 'us' but how the world looks to people with disabilities.... It's about what disability can provide to the listener, not what the listener can do despite disability."[48] Ibby Grace, for example, discusses the various ways music has given her a distinct mode of expression, has structured her perception of others, and has facilitated the writing process.[49]

By rejecting the assumption that the only way to interpret musical listening or hearing is through the lens of the "normal listener," or what Iyer has called the "myth of the solitary listener," theorists such as Straus and Iyer clear a space within which alternative forms of musical subjectivity can emerge. Shared musical experience need not amount to an erasure of difference. Rather, musicking can grant someone access to knowledge about a fellow human being, not through a mirror or normalizing lens that enforces the line between normal and abnormal but in ways that reveal and celebrate difference.

Another way in which recognizing difference can be productive and transformative is through musical performance. Some of these performances may occur in private settings, between family members and friends, and thus be far less formal, more intimate, and unknown to others. (One thinks of Kate's relationship to her music teacher and her father and of the knowledge they had of her abilities, desires, and joys through her performances.) Other performances may be on the public stage (literally and figuratively) and hence reach a wider audience and have a greater reach in transforming perceptions of disability. The performances of groups such as the interPLAY

Orchestra, Flame, and Heavy Load, all of which include musicians with intellectual disabilities, embody the power that music has to express freedom and creativity and are imbued with energy, engagement, and vitality.[50]

Yet it is also important to recognize that disabled people often need others to assist them in musicking, whether they are "access providers," strategic planners, or facilitators.[51] As Giles Perring explains, "the manner in which nondisabled people approach the task of facilitating or collaborating in creative work by artists with learning disabilities has a crucial bearing on the extent that learning-disabled experience and subjectivity is articulated."[52] This speaks directly to the question of epistemic authority and *how* and *why* musical encounters take place. In Perring's study of non-disabled artists involved in these arts-and-disability projects, he found a variety of approaches, some more bound to therapeutic and normalizing methods than others.[53] Ultimately, Perring emphasizes the value of the countercultural approach: "If art can act as a means of constructing the self, then the subjectification, rather than objectification, of all the artists in an arts-and-disability project must be facilitated."[54] This claim highlights the importance of approaching such musical encounters, not with the aim of studying an object but as reflexive and potentially transgressive moments open to the possibility of challenging "mainstream cultural and aesthetic precepts and views about disability."[55] If artists and facilitators adopt this approach, such encounters have the potential to affirm and enable flourishing: "The approaches adopted by nondisabled artists and arts facilitators challenge the dominant institutional role of the learning-disabled person as 'service user.' Within artistic traditions that have valorized alternatives to the hegemony of technique in virtuosic and conservatory traditions, arts practitioners have found the basis for an affirmation of the personhood of learning-disabled people, a personhood fuller than the one constructed for them outside the arts project."[56] In this regard, then, musicking can contribute the sonification of a fuller sense of personhood, perhaps lending a new meaning to the term *personification*.

Remaining Epistemological Questions

In this chapter, I have argued that musical encounters of many kinds can have epistemic moral force, namely, that they can yield knowledge that is morally relevant to how certain individuals are understood, perceived, and valued. Yet many questions remain when considering the ways in which musical encounters can be revelatory and epistemically significant. First, what is the precise nature of this knowledge? It can be about many different things: the very existence of a *musical life* in the broadest sense; a specific capacity or form of musical cognition, emotion, or preference; a particular kind of "hearing," performing, or composing. And it may also be revelatory of *non-musical* dimensions of the person. For example, how can shared musical experience contribute to knowledge about various categories and models of disability and challenge assumptions about disability as a lived experience? The reflections in this chapter have just begun to broach these issues, and though they have been addressed in other fields as well (including music therapy, musicology, music cognition, and disability studies), philosophers of disability have an important role to play in this dialogue.

Second, it is crucial to ask *how* this knowledge is produced: where, through what means, and by whom? How is the musical encounter initiated, and what are its effects? It is undeniably possible for musical subjects to be objectified in the process of musicking and in *philosophizing about* musical experience, so it is important to ask, how do power relations and forms of oppression such as racism, sexism, classism, and ableism shape musical encounters, and how can these dynamics be avoided and resisted? If we acknowledge that the knowledge yielded through various forms of sonification is not necessarily neutral, what does it mean to claim its moral relevance?

These concerns raise the important question of what the purpose of shared musical experience is. What underlies the desire to better know a fellow musical subject? Is there a danger that the musical encounter becomes simply another venue for objectification, whereby the musical subject is reduced to an object of inquiry? To say that sharing a musical experience with someone else *can* yield valuable knowledge about a fellow musical subject does not ensure that this knowledge is accurate or desirable or that it should be shared with others. Clearly, not all musical encounters need to have this epistemic aim; in fact, one element of musicking that can be particularly significant is simply sharing in *music itself* rather than focusing on the participants and any knowledge one might gain about them.

Finally, if philosophers of disability are going to consider and take seriously the musical lives of people with intellectual disabilities because they have significant moral epistemic value, how should they gain access to this knowledge? As the foregoing questions suggest, this can be a fraught endeavor. Though I made the case that expanding philosophical attention to include the musical lives of the intellectually disabled can be an important move, there is no guarantee that the musical portraits that emerge will not fall prey to some of the same problematic dynamics that are evident in other philosophical discussions and arguments about intellectual disability.[57] Engaging in *philosophical sonification*—the work of reflecting on the nature and value of shared musical experience by philosophers of disability—must be done with care, and critical questions regarding power, ableism, humility, and expertise must remain in the foreground.

I have argued that musical experience can be a form of sonification insofar as it facilitates new forms of recognition between individuals, and in this way, it can have epistemic moral force. Yet both the *content* and the *mode* of recognition are important here. Sharing in musical experience can be an opportunity to recognize the other as a fellow human being. This can occur across cultures, trans-generationally, and between individuals who may not live in the world in the same ways or communicate through the same means. These moments of recognition may happen between performer or composer and the audience, between co-performers, and between fellow beholders of a musical event. Yet there can also be oppressive modes of recognition: the enfreakment of the other, the exploitation of differences, or the use of the other simply as a mirror through which my own image is reflected back. However, as I have suggested, the recognition of a fellow musical subject *can* be humanizing if it is done by respecting and embracing difference. In the case of intellectual disabilities, musicking can reveal robust and complex musical lives that directly challenge dehumanizing assumptions and practices. In this way, musical encounters can sonify, and *per*sonify musical subjects in all of their uniqueness, particularity, and personhood and thus can have profound epistemic moral force.

4

Wordlessness Is Not Worldlessness

A Lyrical Interlude

In her book *Lyric Philosophy*, Canadian philosopher, poet, and musician Jan Zwicky differentiates "lyric thought" from mainstream Western analytic philosophy and sees it as a rich possibility for philosophizing. To embrace the lyrical, she says, is to recognize that there is meaning beyond language, to acknowledge that language can limit and restrict, not just assist, our understanding: "philosophy may assume lyric form when it attempts to give voice to an ecology of experience. Under such circumstances, it is not useful to distinguish between art and philosophy."[1] Her call is to enlarge our philosophical imagination, to think of resonance, and to embrace the musical and extralinguistic dimensions of our experience. What might a more lyrical philosophy of intellectual disability mean?

Loss as Gain

A subsidiary aim of the great systems of Western European philosophy has been to secure the world from loss. Lyric allows us to see the whole in the particular; and in so doing, to bring the preciousness, which is the losability, of the world into clear focus.

So the two—lyric thought and the aim of philosophical security—are reconciled only in that moment when the world is secured by the act of relinquishing it. . . . The idea would be not to confront this [possibility of loss], but to come to exist, ourselves, as that possibility.[2]

What does it mean to exist *as the possibility of loss*? Music is temporal; its melodies, rhythms, movements, and harmonies are fleeting. Every musical performance, every shared musical experience, is temporary. Musical worlds exist with the ever-present possibility of loss. They are, in fact, structured by silence, by the absence or loss of sound. Zwicky writes that the world is secured by the act of relinquishing that very security; a similar paradox resides in musical experience, insofar as in order to experience the ontological security that the musical work or performance might offer, we can only experience it as passing, and ultimately, we must relinquish it. And yet music leaves a trace—in silences and in memory, it persists.

We all exist *as the possibility of loss*. The precarity and vulnerability of our existence can be understood as living with the *possibility of loss*, with the *losability* of what is precious to us. This human truth is one that many disabled people know intimately and live with and through on a daily basis. But the "temporarily abled" too often consider disability as synonymous with loss and believe themselves impervious to both. According to this view, disability signifies global loss, not just of function, of form, but of autonomy, value, agency, desire, flourishing, possibility, personhood. And yet ...

Disability is generative, productive, positive; it expresses the richness and complexity of existence.[3] It is experienced not as loss but as fullness, not as what is lacking but as what is present. Of her daughter Sesha, Eva Kittay writes: "It is through my daughter's bodily limitations and her mental incapacities, not despite them, that I experience my daughter as a person—and, in more mystified terms, as a soul. In fact, what I see in her by means of her body is a beautiful soul. . . . There is no one else I have ever met who makes me utter 'soul' as much as this person whose self so fully appears to be her body."[4]

Wordlessness

> Compared with music, all communication by words is shameless; words dilute and brutalize; words depersonalize.[5]

Music can take us beyond the limits of language. Words and language have the power to wound, to do violence, to restrict and reduce, to fail to attend to the specificity of the individual, to obscure personhood, to de-*personalize*.

> It is doubly mistaken, then, to assume that a certain way of using language . . . captures all that is true, or significant, or meaningful in human experience.[6]

> Music is not a defective language.... Lyric meaning does not have the form of linguistic meaning. It is different both in kind and scope.[7]
>
> Lyric thought is a direct response to the fact that the particular capacity for language-use possessed by our species cuts us off from the world in a way, or to a degree, that is painful. We experience the burden of our capacity for language as loss—though we rarely recognize that this is the burden, that what we have lost is silence. Lyric art is the fullest expression of the hunger for wordlessness.[8]

Zwicky reverses what is often the traditional assumption about the primacy of language over silence. In many contexts, wordlessness has been interpreted as pathology, burden, or loss. Yet the lyrical dimensions of our experience reveal that it is the *hunger* for wordlessness and the *burden* of language that we experience as loss. To recover silence, to acknowledge what language obscures, and to accept a desire for wordlessness is to dwell in a different space in which the *musical we* is possible.

People with "profound intellectual disabilities" are often defined by the absence of words, of language. This perpetual silence may be imagined and experienced by those of us who are dependent upon words as a tragic loss. Our views of disability are too binary. Instead of remaining fixed within the distinction between verbal and nonverbal, we should recognize the vast range of expression—not just between people, classes, intellectual ability, and educational background but also at different stages in the life cycle.

Perhaps it is the language user who is diminished in relying solely on language; it is our linguistic world that masks a deeper yearning. In embracing the lyrical, we recognize wordlessness and silence, not as voids to be filled and absences to be mourned but as an embodied space of beginnings, of nourishment, of gesture, of human connection. In speaking about his twenty-five-year-old son Joey, who "has never spoken a word," Stephen Unwin writes, "One way through, I have discovered, is to recognise that presence itself is a speech act. And so I always insist that Joey attends all meetings about his future: it's not that I'm expecting him to suddenly start talking, it's that his very presence articulates the indisputable fact of his existence."[9]

Language, not silence, may be the burden; wordlessness is what we desire. And then silence can become sound. As Evelyn Glennie says, "Silence in music has the potential to be the most profound sound of all that binds us together. I believe we listen to silence differently—the attention is more personal and yet binding, whereby both audience and performer change physically and mentally. . . . Silence engulfs the whole being. The body can present any stance whilst respecting silence as a sound, and the audience will accept the chosen stance."[10]

Wordlessness Is Not Worldlessness

. . . a habitable world: a world that wants me in it.[11]

Only when we have traveled to each other's "worlds" are we fully subjects to each other.[12]

Music can create worlds without words. The sonic landscape that envelops, that moves, is populated by gestures, movements, sounds, expressions. These musical worlds resist explicit or precise definition; their boundaries are porous and mutable, their size indeterminate, their populations varied, their temporal existence transient. Musical worlds can simultaneously be made, shared, and received; they can create habitable spaces for those who, for whatever reason, may not share in discursive, text-based, linguistic worlds. To enter into a musical world, in musical time, is to partake in a relationship—to oneself and one's senses and physical responses and to fellow musical subjects. World travel and play in Maria Lugones's sense of the terms[13] are possible through the subjective experience of musical pieces, forms, moments, performances, and recordings.

A musical world—whether it is of one's own creation or created by others, constituted by a musical work, a cultural tradition, a musical moment, inhabited either alone or with others—can envelop, comfort, agitate, provoke, and energize. It is a world in motion, a world with its own temporality, available to those who hear, see, and feel it. Its boundaries, the price of entry, need not be exclusive; it welcomes its subjects, grants them asylum, joins them to others.

Gesture and the Incalculable

In what manner does feeling impart itself? Partially, but only very partially, it can be transposed into thoughts, that is, into conscious presentations. . . . There always remains in this area of feeling, however, an indissoluble remainder. Language, that is, the concept, is concerned solely with what is soluble. . . . The other two sorts of imparting are instinctive through and through, without consciousness and yet functionally purposive. These are the languages of gesture and of tone.[14]

For me this musical phrase is a gesture. It insinuates itself into my life. I adopt it as my own. Life's infinite variations are essential to our life. And so too even to the habitual character of life. What we regard as expression consists in incalculability.[15]

Embodied musical worlds are made up of gesture and tone. They are dynamic spaces in which bodyminds[16] of all kinds may be present, intermingling, musicking through their individual forms of movement, engaging in modes of expression that eschew the *normal*, exceed the quantifiable and the calculable, subvert the soluble.

Mystery

[A problem is] something which I meet, which I find completely before me, which I can lay seize to and reduce; [a mystery is] something in which I am myself involved, and it can therefore only be thought of as a sphere where the distinction between what is in me and what is before me loses its meaning and initial validity.[17]

The notion that music is that which moves beyond what is expressible in language, that points to something *beyond* what is definable within the confines of philosophy, is echoed in Gabriel Marcel's characterization of his own relationship to music as a philosopher. This is captured in the distinction Marcel draws between a problem and a mystery. How can philosophy retain the mysterious in philosophizing about music? How can philosophers resist transforming *others* into problems to be solved? To engage with the lyrical is to embrace all modes of *being-with* that are dynamic, humble, and open and that do not attempt to fix, solve, resolve, or transform. Musicking with fellow musical subjects can create a *musical we* that does not attempt to normalize, to modify or cure; musical encounters can open a space where musical subjects, in their sameness and difference, communicate and dwell together.

Nor is a world generated by music itself simply a problem to be solved. Though I am intimately bound up in it, elements of this musical world remain mysterious, beyond my grasp. I struggle to give voice in words to my musical encounter; concepts and theories fail to capture the richness and significance of my musical experience. Yet what might it mean to say, as Marcel does, that this distinction between what is in me and what is before me loses meaning? My perception of music is *internal*, my response to it is *mine*, as a musical witness. As one who makes music, it is a sonic, rhythmic, unfolding world that I simultaneously inhabit and create.

For those who are assumed to be "wordless," as well as for those of us who bear the burden of language, lie musical worlds where we can appear, engage, dance and sway, sing, move ourselves and others, live musical lives, and invite others to share in these musical worlds. Wordlessness is not worldlessness.

5
The "Musical We"

To be wise is to be able to grasp another form of life without abandoning one's own; to be able to translate experience into and out of two original tongues. To resist, then, translation that understands itself as a form of reduction.[1]

Shared musical experience can foster the emergence and recognition of fellow human subjects in distinct ways. Rather than simply viewing the "humanizing effect" of musical encounters as a mode of recognizing sameness, I have argued that it is possible, and in fact imperative, to recognize what one has in common with another *through* difference. In this chapter, I will explore how these musical encounters can establish connections between individuals and communities, create and transform relationships, and enable particular modes of being-with. In his Levinasian analysis of music and ethical responsibility, Jeff Warren writes, "Music can be a time and place of sameness for the encounter of another person. Whether musicians improvising together, audience members coming into proximity with each other, or a mother singing to her child, music becomes a time and place where separated humans share a sameness in proximal encounter. What arises in this experience is the demand to respond to the other who is encountered."[2] So how do we respond to these musical others? And what exactly are we sharing by virtue of our proximity within this musical world?

Defining the "Musical We"

In "Making Music Together," phenomenologist Alfred Schutz calls the intersubjective experience of sharing in music making the "musical we." Though his primary focus is on the "we" that is established between performers, I use this term to refer to the relationships established across many different groups of musicking subjects and ask: How is the musical we established? How do configurations of the musical we differ depending on whether it is

Shared Musical Lives. Licia Carlson, Oxford University Press. © Oxford University Press 2022.
DOI: 10.1093/oso/9780197618356.003.0006

established between co-performers, co-witnesses, or performer and witness? And how and why does this musical we have moral force?

In chapter 1, I offered a brief taxonomy of musical others who populate musical encounters, and it is because of their existence and the intersubjective nature of musical experience that sharing in music has ethical significance. Chapter 3 established that musical encounters can yield morally relevant information about fellow musical subjects and their lives, yet the focus of the discussion still maintained a separation between self and other. By moving into a deeper examination of shared musical worlds, I hope to reveal various dimensions of the relationships *between* musical subjects and consider what is distinctive about the musical we as a way of being with others.

Consider the relationship between performers. In playing an instrumental piece with others, I engage in a distinct kind of conversation with them. It is nonverbal yet expressive; it trades in musical motifs, harmonies, melodies, and rhythms rather than concepts and words; it is an embodied dialogue that requires a level of engagement that may be both cognitive and emotional. I perceive musical cues in sound and in gesture, and as the music unfolds, we speak in our own distinct voices while taking part in a sonic dialogue that at once includes each of us yet exceeds our individual parts. Schutz describes the rich texture of this relationship between performers as follows: "Each of them has to, therefore, take into account what the other has to execute in simultaneity. He has not only to interpret his own part, which remains necessarily fragmentary, but he has also to anticipate the other player's interpretation of his—the other's—part and, even more, the other's anticipations of his own execution."[3] Schutz says this shared experience constitutes "the mutual tuning-in relationship, the experience of the 'We,' which is at the foundation of all possible communication."[4] In inhabiting this musical we, I recognize the presence of the other, and this recognition shapes and transforms my relationship to the other. Within this dialogical space of musical unfolding, there is a recognition that all voices are present and must be given their proper due.

While Schutz focuses on how performers establish a musical we, other relationships can also enable a "mutual tuning-in," generating their own forms of the musical we. Between performer and audience, witnesses may recognize performers as creative, expressive subjects who, in sharing their musical performance, are imparting a kind of musical gift.[5] At the same time, there are ways in which the audience members shape the encounter, generating a distinctive performance that envelops and connects witnesses and performers. In her discussion of early Black women blues artists, for example, Angela Davis speaks about the subtle ways in which these women's performances were political. Despite many interpretations of their songs as conforming to certain conventional ideas of women's roles, Davis argues that, in fact, they were engaged in cultivating a space of resistance of which the audience, through call and response, was a crucial part.[6]

The musical we can also exist between co-witnesses of a musical performance. Insofar as they are simultaneously a part of a musical work that is unfolding in time, they are partaking in a distinct temporal world together. As with the connection established between performers, and between audience and performer, co-witnesses, too, share in the experience of moving beyond themselves and inhabiting a shared musical space that is both physical and sonic. In considering these elements of musical encounters more closely, we can look at how the musical we might be significant for relationships with and between people with intellectual disabilities.

Sharing in Musical Time and Space

Music has been called the most temporal of all the arts because it is an art form that necessarily unfolds in time.[7] As Kathleen Higgins has argued, it is the consonance between musical time and one's own temporal existence that creates a sense of existential security.[8] And yet musical experience can also complicate and even disrupt typical notions of a linear unfolding of time, hence the distinction between chronological and musical time. Yet in what ways do these temporal features of music contribute to the constitution of the musical we? Certainly for co-performers, they must tune into this musical time in order to successfully play a piece together. And musical witnesses can also be transported from ordinary clock time into musical time, which may or may not be shared by the performers.

This shared temporal landscape can also offer forms of connection and expression for individuals who, according to other normative measures, could not "share time" in this way. Thus, entering into musical time can be profoundly liberating and provide the basis for connection with others for individuals who do not otherwise conform, in their physical or cognitive activities, to normalized temporal expectations, who do not live easily or comfortably in "ordinary time." In partaking in a musical performance, one marks the passage of musical time, taking up a new rhythm of existence and experiencing time in a way that is distinct from the temporal demands and markers that dictate daily activities and functions.[9]

In the case of intellectual disability specifically, this *shared* musical temporality may be particularly significant. As discussed in chapter 2, there are many ways in which intellectual disability is defined by standards that have a temporal element. The musical world introduces its own time, however; it is one that can be shared in through rhythmic gestures, movement, dance, and song by performer and witness alike. For people whose bodies and minds do not conform to "normal time," partaking in musical time can be a refuge, providing an alternative to what may be viewed from the outside as a failure or inability to conform to the temporal exigencies of living in the world. Insofar as we share in musical time with another person, there is the possibility that neither participant is "behind"; we can achieve a simultaneity that joins us in this shared experience, whether through our movements, bodily rhythms, vocalizations, or expressions.

When we share in a musical experience with others, we are also inhabiting a shared musical space. The physical spaces may be varied; depending on the nature of the encounter, this may happen in a formal setting (e.g., a concert hall), in informal and domestic settings, in institutional settings (whether they are educational spaces, specifically musical spaces, or, for some people with various cognitive or intellectual disabilities, in residential facilities), or virtually, as we experienced in a variety of ways during the pandemic. There is no question that the surroundings alter the experience of the music and are a determining factor in how and why these musical encounters occur. But in what ways are these musical spaces *ethical* spaces that can enable the musical we?

Warren argues that "Music, as something shared with others, becomes a site of proximal encounters with others wherein ethical responsibilities emerge. In music, what is shared is an acoustic space as well as an experience whose meaning is negotiated."[10] Physical proximity in the form of shared musical space can be significant for people who have been sequestered and physically marginalized. Living in institutional settings can rob one of a sense of both agency and joy, and thus to share in musical encounters in such spaces can be transformative.[11] Jeffrey Kittay speaks about how in his daughter Sesha's residential space, soundscapes dominate in various ways, sometimes in ways that are distressing. Yet when music is provided based on Sesha's own preferences, and can shape the contours of her experience of space, sound, and time, these can be profoundly important.[12]

Access to music, even when mediated by a professional, need not be cast within a therapeutic, normalizing model.[13] As we saw in chapter 2, places like Daniel's Music Foundation, a musical space in New York City devoted to enabling and cultivating musical encounters for people with disabilities, can offer a distinctive form of musical asylum, the kind Tia DeNora speaks of: a space of communion, musical joy, and flourishing.[14] And within this space, all the musical collaborators can shape and inhabit a musical we whose goal is communion and "mutual tuning-in," rather than the cure, erasure, or overcoming of a particular condition.[15]

Musical worlds founded on the premise of musical joy and flourishing can also generate a sense of what Higgins has called "ontological security." Drawing from R. D. Laing's work, she argues that music, through both its physiological effects and what she calls its "vitality effects,"[16] confers upon individuals this ontological security: an ontologically secure person "has a 'centrally firm sense' that he or she has the same ontological status as other people. . . . [T]he person senses that he or she occupies the same order of being as other people and shares the encountered world with them. . . . On the basis of this conviction, the person feels confident of living in a *shared* world, whatever his or her articulate views about the nature of that world or that sharing might be."[17] Thus, in addition to sharing in the musical performance itself, being *present* with others in this musical world can create a form of being-with that offers a distinct form of assurance that may otherwise be absent. There are many ways one can feel confident in living in a shared world with others. And yet for individuals who do not inhabit normative bodies or minds, opportunities to engage in activities that serve as the foundation for sharing in a world are often limited by structural barriers, social exclusion, and marginalization. Here musical encounters can offer a basis for such ontological security and companionship.[18]

Shared Musical Joy and Mutual Flourishing

In addition to sharing in musical time and spaces, a third dimension of this shared musical experience is what Higgins terms "musical joy." In the case of being co-witnesses, one can share in this joy of a musical performance with another individual and thus find a point of connection in this third term. Consider Eva Kittay's description of Sesha's enjoyment of music:

Even a seemingly devastating cognitive impairment, such as my daughter's, may allow for an intensity in enjoyment that most of us miss. My daughter's appreciation of music is such that at times she can hardly contain her joy. Would she enjoy it more if she had the intellectual ability to understand exactly how the music is constructed, the form of a sonata, the distinctive lines of a fugue? Perhaps. Or perhaps not. Perhaps that is a different and not inherently superior way of enjoying music. When it comes to the role of music in a flourishing life, as far as I can conceive of a flourishing life, she has at least one element of it in spades. The caveat is that without the appropriate social environment, that capacity might not be recognized or encouraged. She needs me to turn the music on for her. Her flourishing may therefore be more precarious, but it is no less fulsome.[19]

Kittay's description of Sesha's enjoyment raises a number of important questions that speak directly to the nature of musical engagement itself. It also points to potential challenges for those claiming that people with profound disabilities cannot share in musical joy in the way that others can. First, must musical joy be based on a cognitive understanding of the musical work itself? It seems clearly not in Sesha's case. Yet this is not unique to persons with intellectual disabilities; it is fairly obvious that the enjoyment of music for millions of people does not rest upon their understanding of the mechanics and nuances of the music itself. The three aspects of shared experience I have been discussing—shared time, space, and joy—suggest that there are important dimensions of the shared musical encounter that do not necessarily rely on an interpretive stance, a shared understanding of the musical work itself. (Note that this is different from the ways in which co-performers rely on a shared knowledge and mutual interpretation of a musical work.) While forms of musical knowledge and understanding of the specific work *may* shape the experience for some witnesses, the ethical import of musical encounters is not grounded in a specific kind of musical perception or musical knowledge. One can share in modes of musical appreciation in ways that are meaningful and ethically salient without having to engage in and/or share a particular interpretation of the musical work.[20] To claim that the value of music relies on a particular kind of cognitive engagement with it is to deny the possibility of a broader shared experience. This is problematic insofar as it instantiates modes of exclusion and narrows the scope of philosophical consideration of a wide range of listeners and witnesses.

Second, there is the question of *how* one knows whether the other person is, in fact, enjoying the musical encounter and "sharing" in it in the way that I am. Music therapist Gary Ansdell considers the epistemic challenges posed by establishing that someone who does not speak is able to share in a musical experience. In discussing the example of one client, Mary, he describes her facial expressions, her laughter in response to the music, and her participation in making music with him. Thus, even though she is not able to offer a verbal description of her enjoyment, Ansdell says:

> She clearly follows the structure of the song and attends closely for the precise moment in it that calls for her hand to reach out and strike the bell. But more than this, I also have the sense of Mary's living through the melody of this song, then taking the musical invitation to add her part in just that musical time and space. I also feel her sensing my living through this melody as I sing it, sharing musical time and space with me. A musical experience has been given and received (both ways), something that connects us closely for these minutes.[21]

Ansdell's characterization here points to a mutual, reciprocal exchange that occurs, though the encounter is experienced within a therapeutic relationship.

Yet there is also a way in which the experience of sharing music with someone else, regardless of the participants' respective abilities, exceeds what any linguistic description of this shared musical joy can capture. This can be true whether individuals are sharing in a musical performance as co-witnesses or co-performers, and performers can sense the audience's enjoyment of a performance though they may not be literally giving voice to these sentiments. Ansdell calls this co-subjectivity, when "my pleasure is enhanced by knowing other members of the audience are simultaneously experiencing this too."[22] In fact, one might argue that linguistic characterizations of these shared moments in language will always be impoverished to some extent; recall Nietzsche's claim that, compared with music, "words depersonalize."

There can also be a close relationship between musical joy and flourishing. Eva Kittay discusses the relationship between these two dimensions of musicking in speaking about Sesha's musical life. Her description of Sesha's musical joy is particularly significant in that it challenges the assumption held by some philosophers that individuals like Sesha are incapable of any meaningful sense of flourishing.[23] Though Sesha needs someone else to enable this form of musical joy, and thus her flourishing is precarious in distinct ways, *all* musical subjects, to varying degrees, depend in some way on others for their experience of music and musical joy. *Inter*dependence is at the heart of musicking and musical flourishing.

Transforming and Transposing Relationships

Sharing in a musical experience with others can forge new ways of being-with; in this way, not only can music be transformative for individuals themselves and the ways they are perceived by others, but it can also reconfigure relationships between persons. In the context of intellectual disability, these transpositions can be significant. What was once assumed to be an asymmetrical relationship in certain settings can become reciprocal or even reversed, allowing a new "we" to emerge. This can happen with co-performers, performer and audience, and co-witnesses of a musical performance. The musical we can also be transformative in that it reverses or transcends certain binaries and power dynamics that exist beyond the musical encounter.[24]

One assumption that is challenged by the musical we is the passive/active binary. As performers, composers, or witnesses of musical performances, people with intellectual disabilities may emerge as fully engaged subjects in a world that often denies their full personhood. Musical expression can serve as a means of communication, and by sharing in musical experience, they can possess an equally commanding presence and partake in a reciprocal exchange. In this musical context, the person can be an engaged witness or performer, actively musicking with others. As John Vorhaus describes it, music "allows for communion between listeners, and between players and listeners. A favoured melody, rhythm, or sound world is food for the soul, and allows one person to reach out to or connect with another. This is why music can remind us of someone's humanity and contribute to a sense of human fellowship—two themes repeatedly discussed by those who write about profound disability and those who live with it."[25] In these musical contexts, people with intellectual disabilities are active, rather than passive, subjects. And their participation in musical encounters opens the possibility for mutual exchange, enabling forms of reciprocity that serve as the basis for a human connection.

In addition to problematizing the way the active/passive binary often corresponds to the able/disabled dichotomy, musical encounters can also disrupt the line between normal and abnormal, a value dualism that so often dominates philosophical discussions of disability. If we move away from the medicalized context of pathology, away from the deficit and personal tragedy models of disability, into the realm of the arts and musical experience, lines between the normal and the pathological can shift or disappear.[26]

But how exactly does the musical we disrupt these boundaries? First, insofar as there is a commitment to a shared experience, musical encounters can draw participants out of the roles they may otherwise be expected to inhabit, roles that reinforce the boundary between "normal and abnormal" or "able and disabled." To say this is not to suggest that an individual's disability disappears; rather, it is to acknowledge that there are modes of being-with that are not necessarily bound by externally imposed categories and designations. Second, because the musical nature of the shared experience may not rely on skills, capacities, or expectations that otherwise structure an individual's life along imposed lines of demarcation (able/disabled), there is the possibility of sharing in modes of enjoyment and exchange that are grounded upon different practices, kinds of expressions, and abilities. Finally, I am not suggesting that all aspects of one's identity somehow disappear in musical encounters; there may be ways in which what is typically valorized as "normal" gives way to alternative modes of being that are worthy of celebration and may actually be *preferable* in a musical context. Insofar as these might encompass features that are associated with an individual's disability, the musical we may allow these non-normative aspects of a person to flourish and be celebrated.

The musical we can disrupt existing relationships and create new ones through various kinds of role reversals that can happen through musical encounters. In "Musical Becoming," I explore three specific "reversals" whereby people with intellectual disabilities become active musical subjects as composers, performers, and listeners. Whereas these individuals are often assumed to be mere passive spectators or recipients of therapy, when we consider the many ways in which they can inhabit these multiple musical roles, they become musical agents sharing their musical gifts with others. Whether it is in the intimate setting of a shared song at home with a family member or a more formal performance or composition, the broad range of musicking that can occur is further confirmation of the rich relationships that can exist and be nourished by sharing in a musical world.[27]

Musical Presence

In his book *On Presence: Variations and Reflections*, existentialist philosopher and theologian Ralph Harper describes presence this way: "When I think of presence, I think of what it is like for the soul to be touched, the mystery of the whole self, body and spirit. . . . Presence can be explosive, liberating, revealing, quieting. Presence has force and authority. . . . It is not monism or dualism; it is a unitary experience and an experience of totality in the midst of shattering differences."[28] This human desire to connect with others, to establish a "we" that transcends traditional dichotomies and fosters new forms of connection, often happens in encounters with those who possess certain unique or unexpected qualities. Harper writes: "Indeed, we sometimes feel we are in the presence of someone qualitatively different from others, and we remember their quality long after they have gone from us. They affect us differently from those who are closed to us. With them and through them we seem to leave the subject-object world of epistemology and penetrate a land of participation, acceptance, understanding. Nevertheless, strictly speaking, presence is always an approximation of our longing for an end to barriers."[29] In a sense, the musical we can be understood as a response to this longing, to the desire to partake in presence, to recognize another and to *be* recognized. Sharing in musical space and time can establish a very different basis for such encounters, and simply by *being there* together, whether as witnesses, co-performers, or givers and recipients of musical gifts, certain structural, architectural, and attitudinal barriers can recede.

Harper also recognizes that the arts, and music specifically, can provide the occasion for experiencing presence. Music, he says, "is a series of impressions of sound, as evanescent as can be, far more than the painting that will be around long after the instruments or the machine have stopped playing. And yet no more powerful impression of presence reaches most people than through music."[30] However, he goes on to say that in art, we are somehow more comfortable with these encounters than we are in real life; these impressions of presence in art, he says, "demand little of us, and leave no scars, no questions. This is virtual presence, not real presence. [S]ince art is mirror and illusion, there is nothing permanent to respond to. One can only respond to what can return the favor. All art can offer is a reminder of immediacy of reality; it cannot offer reality. That is why art is ultimately unsatisfying; we are left to our own solitude, unless relieved by a real, not a virtual, presence."[31] I do not know if Harper was inspired by the work of Emanuel Levinas, but Levinas makes a similar argument in an early essay, "Art and Reality." He argues that art offers a means of evasion, rather than demanding from us a confrontation with reality.[32] Yet the characterization of the experience of art as simply a "virtual encounter" assumes that the musical encounter is disembodied, that it is an encounter with sound alone. But the activity of musicking, where we witness another musical subject performing, playing, sharing in the music in some way, where we engage in the kind of "mutual tuning-in," is not merely virtual presence but *real* presence. This is a mode of concretely being with others that simultaneously establishes the possibility of moving beyond ourselves. This "relief" of real presence, as Harper characterizes it, *is* possible in embodied, temporal, dynamic musical encounters of the kind I have been exploring. The musical we need not constitute an evasion, a virtual or less real form of connection; rather, it can *affirm* the presence, mystery, being, reality, and the call of a fellow musical subject. As Daniel Barenboim has said, we paradoxically both find ourselves and lose ourselves in music.[33]

Musical Virtues

Returning to Peter Kivy's discussion in "Musical Morality," recall that the third kind of moral force he defines is music's "character-building" force. In Platonic terms, one could speak of the effects that musical modes and harmonies have on the soul and the ways it can shape one's character, cultivating virtue or encouraging vice. Kivy's focus is specifically on the musical work itself and whether absolute music has the power to affect one's behavior and character. I share Kivy's skepticism about musical works, simply by virtue of their rhythms, harmonies, modes, and other musical characteristics, being able to directly affect one's moral character. Yet I do think *shared musical experience* can have moral force in this way, particularly through the cultivation of virtues.[34]

Before considering specific virtues, however, a few qualifications are necessary. First, the virtues I consider are by no means exclusively tied to musical experience, nor do I want to argue that musical encounters will *necessarily* promote these virtues. Moreover, the possibility of cultivating them differs greatly depending on various factors, including the roles of the individuals involved, the relationship between them, and the material and structural context in which these musical encounters occur. Finally, the four virtues I address here are not the *only* virtues that are relevant to the musical encounter.[35] I have chosen to focus on these four—empathy, acknowledged dependence humility, and solidarity—because they are especially significant in the context of shared musical experiences with intellectually disabled persons.

Higgins argues that music can cultivate empathy in a number of ways: "Music develops our ability to approach others in a non-defensive, noncompetitive fashion. . . . Our listening stance is a receptive one, and it facilitates identification with others. . . . Enjoyment of music involves the experience of taking satisfaction in a state of mind in which one does not oppose oneself to other human beings."[36] If one witnesses a musical performance, there can be an openness, a receptivity that structures that encounter. In recognizing a performer or fellow witness's engagement and enjoyment, I can take part in it as well. Vijay Iyer echoes this when he writes, "Music perception begins with empathy—perception of another embodied person—mutual embodiment; the capacity for music begins with the capacity to recognize another human being."[37]

But to claim "identification" with others begs for further clarification. Does naming this *empathy* suggest that there is an epistemic component to this identification with another? What is it that one must know, or recognize, about one's fellow audience member or co-performer that constitutes an empathic stance? Higgins suggests it is a shared joy; for jazz musician Garry Hagberg, in the experience of improvisation, it may be the recognition of the other as autonomous and distinct from oneself and as the recipient of one's attentiveness. He explains that we must not attend to another's life "as a mere collection of discrete atomistic actions or events"; rather, "we attend to a life by seeing its teleology, its trajectories of development, where what is now happening came from. [T]he musical case in fact casts light on the ethical: there is something deeply analogous to 'ear training' in the realm of human acknowledgement."[38]

In addition to recognizing certain shared attributes, the musical encounter can foster empathy insofar as individuals are occupying a shared musical space and moving together in musical time, as discussed above. These forms of proximity and presence allow me to be open to the other's experience as well as my own. If we are both performers, I must be attuned to her gestures, her movement, and her musical forms of expression; if we are co-witnesses, her experience of the musical performance and her expressions and responsiveness shape my own experience of the music as well. This kind of "mutual tuning-in" that can happen in musical encounters can hone skills of attunement that may be transferred to other occasions, to non-musical spaces and encounters, and may enhance the range of communication between myself and the other. My capacity for empathy may be enlarged, as musical encounters expand the possibilities of my witnessing certain dimensions of this other person's joys, sorrows, abilities, and vulnerabilities, allowing me to become better attuned to the other's ways of being.[39]

For co-performers, this openness to the other is essential as well. In his discussion of improvisation, Hagberg identifies thirteen virtues, including "respecting complexity and individuality, mutual respect, and attentiveness." One virtue that he highlights in the improvisational jazz encounter is the attention to complexity and context. He writes, "What, jazz improvisation asks, is happening in *this* moment, with *these* people, in *this* setting, under *these* conditions? Given that *this* musical gesture has just been made in *this* circumstance, what is possible *now*? Jazz improvisation indeed shows within its practice how much attention we should give to the complexities of real moral questions, real moral moments, people, settings, conditions, and circumstances."[40] Being open to asking these question can foster greater empathy—the cultivation of our capacity to genuinely witness and engage with another's experience.[41]

Another virtue that can be cultivated through musical encounters is one that philosopher Alasdair MacIntyre has named the virtue of acknowledged dependence. In his book *Dependent Rational Animals*, MacIntyre talks about vulnerability and dependency in relation to our human lives, a point that has been made by many feminist and disability scholars.[42] No one lives a life of complete independence, and the task of theorizing, affirming, valuing, and enabling forms of dependency and interdependence is imperative. So how might musical encounters help in this regard?

If one is a member of a musical ensemble, there are multiple modes of interdependence that structure these encounters. As musicians, we are mutually dependent on each other to achieve the musical result that we desire; harmonically and rhythmically, various voices intersect and sustain, dialogue, and dance in ways that are constitutive of the musical performance. Performers may also be dependent on the conductor, the composer, and the musical score. And finally, as embodied individuals, we rely on our own bodies and instruments to give voice to our musical creations. These multiple dependencies enable our musical lives, but they also make us vulnerable. The musical worlds that we create are precarious and precious, sustained by collective passion, attention, desire, and commitment to these bonds. To acknowledge and respect these interdependencies is to be, in many ways, a virtuous performer. But more broadly, to recognize our shared vulnerabilities, precariousness, and dependence on each other, both musically and beyond, can be a powerful mode of embracing the commonalities shared with and between people with intellectual disabilities.

Just as ensembles and musical performances rely on modes of interdependency, these musical encounters also require a degree of humility. There are many different forms of humility that a musical encounter can provoke: humility in the presence of the beauty of a musical performance, awe in the face of musical talent and expression, a performer's humility in relation to the composer's demands, and even humility in recognizing and appreciating *others'* capacity to be moved. All of these experiences of humility are possible in musical encounters that involve people with intellectual disabilities, whether they are the audience members, performers, or composers. For individuals who have been often denied agency and epistemic authority, the power to express themselves as a part of a musical we, and to have their musical lives and expressions valued, cannot be underestimated.

In writing about the philosophical treatment of people with intellectual disabilities, Kittay argues that epistemic humility is necessary, particularly in view of the ways moral philosophers have made claims about the (absence of) personhood by relying on unrealistic or stipulative definitions of disability.[43] To encounter an individual in a musical setting may bring out certain elements of someone's personhood in ways that are distinctive, that may not have otherwise been evident, and that one may not fully understand. On a theoretical note, to expand philosophy's range to include such examples (especially since they do not involve traditional evaluative measures based on linguistic capacity) can challenge ableist assumptions and allow us to acknowledge our own forms of ignorance.[44] Hagberg emphasizes the importance of "respecting complexity" in jazz improvisation: "we find severely truncated narratives of morally complex situations themselves morally offensive: they fail to take complexity seriously."[45] His argument against the "trivialization of complexity" can equally apply to attenuated and impoverished portraits of "the intellectually disabled." The distinction that Gabriel Marcel has drawn between a problem, "which I can lay seize to and reduce," and a mystery[46] applies here as well. Neither music nor human beings can or should be reduced to a problem to be solved. A stance of humility is one that recognizes the presence and mystery before me in my fellow musical subjects.

In addition to acknowledging our mutual vulnerability and interdependence, the musical encounter can also foster a sense of solidarity.[47] To recognize the possibility of working toward a common end, and sharing in musical joy together, is to affirm the value of one's fellow musical subjects. Levinson writes, "Music is of undeniable value as a sort of social glue and agent of solidarity, helping to create, maintain, and strengthen a sense of community."[48] This sense of solidarity can be present throughout the duration of the musical encounter but can last beyond it as well. Warren speaks about the human dimensions of our musical encounters that exceed them and that leave what he calls "traces" after they have ended. These traces are ethically significant, as they, too, constitute a call upon us: "Music is always linked with human beings, because in creative and experiential acts we leave traces. The 'trace' shows that all musical experience is connected to people and their acts. Second, since our musical experiences leave traces that affect other people, we are responsible to other people in the ways that we create, perform and experience music. The 'trace' links music to ethics and reveals that ethical responsibility is not to music itself, but a responsibility to other people who may be influenced by the trace of my encounter with music."[49] To recognize musical solidarity is to remain committed to those whom we encounter through shared musical experience. In concert with people with intellectual disabilities, partaking in musicking can be experienced as a call: a call to engage together in new modalities, to facilitate more opportunities for musical encounters, to cultivate and sustain musical friendships and dialogues, and to enable mutual flourishing.

Enabling the "Musical We": Cautionary Notes

I firmly believe in the generative and transformative power of the musical we. Yet as Jeff Warren reminds us, "If musical experience requires response to others, then the ways that we use and conceive of music are not ethically neutral."[50] In view of this fact, I am somewhat wary of overstating and romanticizing the musical we or, worse yet, reinscribing the very dynamics that these reflections have attempted to critique and remedy. Here, then, are some considerations moving forward.

Musical encounters can be the basis for assertions, iterations, and performances of the self; yet for many people with intellectual or cognitive disabilities, these occasions must be mediated by non-disabled individuals. As Christian Perring writes when speaking about disability arts projects for people with learning disabilities, "If art can act as a means of constructing the self, then subjectification rather than objectification, of all the artists in an arts-and-disability project must be facilitated."[51] To engage in shared musical experiences means creating the space for *subjectification*, for musical subjects to emerge, rather than engaging in an encounter that objectifies the other. If these shared musical encounters are going to have the potential to contribute to this process of subjectification, some cautionary notes are necessary.

First, it is important to acknowledge that musical experience may not be possible or desirable for everyone. Not everyone enjoys or is capable of enjoying music, and for some, it can be distressing and, worse, cause forms of harm. Though I have been speaking about the virtues and value of establishing a musical we, there is no question that music can be exploited and weaponized to cause harm or distress.[52] In other cases, there may be strong negative associations with a particular kind of music, or music generally may simply amount to personal preference, so it is important not to *pathologize* a dislike of music. In creating shared musical spaces with individuals with intellectual and cognitive disabilities, this can be especially important to recognize, particularly if they are incapable of expressing their preferences and desires—musical or otherwise—clearly. We cannot assume that music has a universally positive effect, nor should it be imposed or inflicted upon others.

Second, I am in no way defending an essentialist claim about the universality of musical experience, nor do I argue that the capacity to engage in or with music is a *necessary* feature of our human condition or of happiness and well-being.[53] While I see value in paying attention to the ways musicking can contribute to flourishing for some individuals with intellectual and cognitive disabilities, I am not simply adding "musical capacity" or "musical enjoyment" to a list of necessary criteria for personhood or flourishing. Moreover, given the complex ways in which certain problematic musical portraits of disability have been perpetuated, I certainly do not mean to romanticize the musical lives and encounters that involve disabled persons.

Finally, musical spaces must be accessible. In establishing various ensembles, various configurations of the musical we, it is important to be attentive to the dynamics that structure these encounters to ensure that they are not undermining, rather than enabling, communication and connections. The modes of recognition and of being-with in the musical we matter on all levels. As Meryl Alper states, the economics and politics of utilizing and celebrating the power of certain kinds of technology to "give voice" are complex and often imbalanced.[54] This is equally true of musical endeavors. Thus, fostering the musical we must involve a consideration of the historical, social, economic, and political conditions that define and enable these encounters and the complex power dynamics and structural, material realities that shape them.

In some cases, musicking will require particular forms of instruments or technologies, and individuals do not have equal access to these. As Michael Watts and Barbara Ridley point out in speaking about the Drake Music Project, a project for individuals with profound disabilities, "The freedom of these musicians to choose and lead a good life through musicianship was constrained by more than the availability of the appropriate resources: it was also held in check by the concern that their music making might be perceived as therapy rather than artistry."[55] Particularly for individuals who are more marginalized and vulnerable, and where access to resources is limited, to recognize the value of sharing in a musical world with others *beyond* a therapeutic or clinical context requires a commitment to creating enabling conditions that will foster these possibilities. Philosophers of disability who are interested in combating ableism and affirming the richness of disabled lives can view this as an opportunity to join this conversation and to further examine the value of the musical we and find ways to enable disability justice through the arts.

Conclusion

Musical Worlds

In presenting a case for the ethical and epistemological significance of shared musical experience, I have explored the ways in which musicking sonifies dimensions of the self, our relationships, and our similarities and differences and creates a "musical we." Though I have focused primarily on disability, these forms of sonification can be meaningful for anyone engaging in music. I have also defended the importance of philosophical sonification, arguing that attending to the musical lives of people with intellectual and cognitive disabilities can be transformative for philosophies of disability. (The title of a talk I gave a few years back, "Why Philosophers Need Music Therapy," might serve as a good subtitle for this task.)

Throughout the book, I have used "musical" as an adjective to describe various phenomena: musical selves, musical lives, musical virtues, musical flourishing, musical virtues. While I have tried to give content and shape to these ideas, there is far more to be said, and not just by philosophers. And so, in the spirit of dialogue across fields, I will conclude with some interdisciplinary questions and connections.

Counterpoint and Harmonies

Many philosophers of music have called for a more historical, contextualized approach to the philosophy of music.[1] Few, however, have identified the value of doing so in the context of disability. Bringing a critical disability lens to the philosophy of music can challenge elements of existing theories and generate new questions. For example, in what ways do philosophers of music posit a "normal" listening subject, and what might departures from this musical *normate* (to borrow Rosemarie Garland Thomson's term) mean?[2] How can including disability in research shape theories regarding music and emotions, music as a language, and phenomenological investigations of musical performance? My experience playing with Nobu Tsujii and the Longwood Symphony confirmed the importance of examining the place of disability in musicking of all kinds, as performers and co-performers and as musical witnesses. As Stefan Honisch so eloquently explains in discussing Tsujii playing Beethoven, if we can acknowledge the expectations we inevitably bring to all of our musical encounters and critically reflect on how our musical bodies engage, perceive, respond, and interact in both expected and unexpected ways, we can recognize the generative potential of shared musical experience and appreciate how musicking can "blur the edges between ability and disability."[3] The embodied, performative, and social dimensions of music can challenge fixed categories and binaries and offer creative forms of resistance.[4]

Insofar as critical disability theory is committed to an intersectional approach, it can make significant contributions to both the philosophy of music and philosophies of disability. Helen Meekosha argues that a paradigm shift is necessary in disability theory. Disability studies has been a predominantly Northern academic endeavor that has failed to account for the experiences, practices, voices, and forms of knowledge produced in the Global South. Many critical issues arise when facing the narrowness and "Northernness" of disability theory, including claims to universality, the erasure of voices, and the centrality of colonization as *producing* forms of impairment, disablement, and suffering.[5] Sami Schalk and Jina B. Kim discuss the ways feminist-of-color disability studies has challenged the whiteness of the field, and they identify important methods and domains of inquiry (including discourse, healthcare, state violence, and activism).[6] These calls for expanding the scope of work in disability studies are equally important in the area of disability arts and disability aesthetics and can inform philosophical work on disability and music by posing critical questions moving forward. What new forms of musicking can be learned from disabled musicians, witnesses, performers, composers, and theorists? How can some of the methodological and philosophical challenges that emerge (e.g., regarding positionality, authority, epistemic injustice) inflect cross-cultural work on music and disability? What does it mean to "decolonize" both philosophies of music and philosophies of disability?

There is also the question of how music therapy and scientific research fit into my call for expanding work on music, philosophy, and disability. Many disabled persons have a complex and often fraught relationship to the rehabilitative and clinical world. Disability theorists, activists, philosophers of disability, and disability bioethicists (myself included) have challenged aspects of the medical model of disability and have exposed and critiqued ableism in these contexts. Others, such as Joseph Straus, have raised concerns about allowing music therapy to be the dominant or sole arena in which disability and music are discussed.[7] Yet dismissing or refusing to engage with these fields and approaches cannot be the answer; rather, critical interdisciplinary engagement and dialogue are vital.

While the medical *model* of disability is problematic, the medical world is an essential part of the lives of many people with disabilities. Moreover, for some individuals with cognitive and intellectual disabilities, music therapy may be their primary mode of accessing music. Though I have argued that it is crucial that opportunities for musicking exist beyond the therapeutic realm, finding the harmonies and dissonances between disability theorists, philosophers of disability, and music therapists has the potential to move all these fields in new directions.[8] Finally, work in the fields of music psychology and music cognition should include the perspectives and musical lives of people with disabilities, as researchers and participants, as this can provide important challenges and contributions to approaches, methods, questions, and conclusions that emerge from these scientific and clinical fields.[9]

Expanding Musical Worlds

In *The Faces of Intellectual Disability*, I explored the historical and philosophical worlds of intellectual disability in an effort to show important and troubling connections between them. In the chapters here, I have considered what it means to inhabit a musical world, both individually and collectively. By entering into these various musical worlds, inviting others to share them with us, and traveling beyond our personal and cultural borders and preferences, new kinds of understanding and connection are possible.

But what does it mean to have access to a particular musical world and for that world to be habitable? The phrase "musical world" can have many meanings. We can speak about how the musical work itself creates a distinct world; a musical world can refer to the private world of an individual's experience of musicking; it can mean sharing a particular musical space in time, including local, virtual, and cultural spaces.[10] In the context of intellectual disability, sharing in musical worlds can challenge erroneous assumptions and can highlight the dangers of privileging cognitive abilities and rational discourse above all else. This is true not just for philosophers and their theories; more concretely, sharing in musicking can be morally expansive and generative. It can grant new forms of what Eva Kittay has called moral access:

> [M]oral access is access to something morally significant in the world. There are times when such significance is entirely transparent to us, when our moral principles guide us in a reliable fashion or when our empathy is already active and we understand how we are to respond. But in situations where another's plight, struggle, or needs go unnoticed, when we are indifferent or unaware of the impact of our actions on those whom we don't recognize as moral equals, we need something—a narrative, a tap on the shoulder—to shake us out of our indifference and to gain something that is more than epistemic access to the other. This is access to what the other cares about and her entitlement or right to have these cares taken into account.[11]

Music, I argue, can play this role; it can reveal what matters to another person and can challenge and disrupt both indifference and ignorance in the face of intellectual and cognitive disability.

Musicking can also reveal latent dimensions of ourselves, foster a basis for communal engagement, and expand possibilities and modes of flourishing. For people with intellectual disabilities, this can be particularly significant. John Vorhaus argues that it is better to err on the side of overestimating another's capacities or potential for participation in a "common life with others" than to wrongly assume certain forms of incapacity.[12] From the most formal to the most mundane and intimate settings, sharing in musical experience can be the basis for a kind of social connection that is vitally important and transformative for all involved.

This call for expanding and valorizing these many musical worlds may strike some as too idealistic. Certainly, music does not offer a solution to all problems, and in some contexts, it can cause great harm. And yet, as I hope this book has confirmed, musicking can improve and transform people's lives immeasurably. I remain deeply hopeful about the value of musical encounters because of their power to sonify so many dimensions of our individual and collective existence. By sharing our musical lives with others, accepting their musical gifts and offering our own, recognizing our similarities and differences, and embracing the musical we, we can make our worlds, musical and otherwise, more habitable and just.

Coda

A Remarkable Serendipity

We name and sing our worlds into existence.
 The amplitudes and frequencies of our words, our songs, become place and time.
  It is utterance given form.

—Jan Swinburne[1]

The central themes of this book—music and sonification—are rooted in sound. Yet musical experience encompasses far more than just hearing and listening. Our presence in musical worlds is embodied, and our engagement with music may be as visual and tactile as it is sonorous. I have focused on the ways in which shared musical experience can sonify dimensions of ourselves and our relationships to others. Yet sonification points to the revelatory power of *translation* more generally. Music is just one art form that can translate and transform experiences, create new worlds, and bring into relief elements of existing worlds.

In searching for an image for the cover of this book, I reached out to the Toronto-based artist Jan Swinburne, whose painting *Six Figures* is on the cover of my book *The Faces of Intellectual Disability*. We were astonished to discover remarkable parallels in our work. In these intervening years, we have both been thinking about similar themes: the creative potential of sonification; the significance of words, voice, and voicelessness; performance as a form of social justice; adaptive technology in the arts; and the importance of place, mystery, and joy in aesthetic experience. Swinburne is an intermedia artist whose work engages with text, sound, music, digital media, sculpture, and video. The piece we chose for this book, *TIME: Wander Lost in the Foothills of Impasto*, is part of an ongoing project called "Waveform Landscapes." Here is how Swinburne describes the project: "the emotive source for this body of work is my voice: spoken words transformed from mind to body to air to digital audio recording to visual rendering through and by machines and then back to handworked objects. . . . The forms depicted are novel but rendered patterns of places that feel familiar. Language is transformed to visual silent voicelessness. . . . The only hint of the word source is held within the title. It is a journey of solidification through materiality and a digital wandering."[2] Based on her utterance of the word "time," Swinburne's waveform sculpture is a unique rendering of the relationship between time, sound, and place. As the cover of this book, it creates a duet between solidification and sonification.

Acknowledgments

Portions of chapter 1 are taken from "Encounters with Musical Others," in *Phenomenology and the Arts*, edited by Licia Carlson and Peter Costello (Lexington Press, 2014). Thank you to the estate of Pablo Neruda and to Farrarr, Straus and Giroux for granting permission to republish an excerpt from "Oda a las cosas," in Pablo Neruda, *Navegaciones y regresos*, © 1959, Pablo Neruda and Fundación Pablo Neruda. Excerpt from "Ode to Things" from *All The Odes: Bilingual Edition*, edited by Ilan Stavans. Translation copyright © 2013 by Ilan Stavans. Reprinted by permission of Farrarr, Straus and Giroux. All Rights Reserved.

This book has had an incredibly long gestation period, and I have many people in my professional, musical, and personal worlds to thank. Many thanks to my editor at Oxford University Press, Norm Hirschy, whose enthusiasm for this project is greatly appreciated, and to the anonymous reviewers who took the time and care to offer such helpful feedback. To Jan Swinburne, thank you for your beautiful artwork, "Time: Wander Lost in the Foothills of Impasto," which graces the cover of this book. This "waveform landscape," capturing the sound of the word "time," is the perfect visual and tactile complement to the idea of sonification.

This book would not have come about if not for the students at the Rehabilitation School in Poughkeepsie, New York, who first gave me a glimpse of what shared musical experience could mean beyond my ordinary musical life. I am deeply grateful for the opportunities I have had to present and publish my work on music and disability, all of which have shaped the evolution of this book. Special thanks to Joseph Straus, Stephanie Jensen-Moulton, Blake Howe, Stefan Honisch, and all the contributors to *The Oxford Handbook of Music and Disability Studies* whose work has deepened my own perspectives on music and disability tremendously; Jane Dryden and the philosophy faculty and students at Mt. Allison University; Christine Dinkins, Steen Halling, and the participants of the International Human Science Research Conference at Wofford College; the participants in the conference at the University of Rhode Island where Peter Costello and I were able to share work from our book *Phenomenology and the Arts*; the

Rhode Island Philosophical Society; the faculty and students at Mount St. Mary and Misericordia University; the panelists at the APA invited symposium, especially Adam Cureton; Ashley Taylor and Kevin McDonough and all the contributors to the special issue of *Philosophical Inquiry in Education*; Matthew Wappett and Kristina Arndt for the invitation to contribute to their foundational text in disability studies.

    I am especially grateful for the work of John Vorhaus, Simo Vehemas, Sophia Wong, Teresa Blankmeyer-Burke, Michael Bérubé, and the countless other philosophers and disability scholars/activists (far too many to name here) who have taught me so much. I am deeply indebted to Eva Kittay for sharing her philosophical wisdom all these years, for our collaborations, and for sharing her beautiful Sesha with me and with so many; to Stephen Unwin, whom I thank for our many zoom conversations, reading drafts, talking theater and art, and introducing me to Joey's and Gabriel's worlds; and to Matthew Murray, who has been a sounding board for so many of my ideas about philosophy, disability, and music and whose collaboration and friendship have been invaluable. Thank you to my colleagues and friends at Seattle University for numerous opportunities to come back to share these ideas. I am especially grateful to Maria Carl, Kate Reynolds, and Pat Burke, and I will never forget the memory of the beautiful Queen Judy. To my beloved NEH Disability Studies family, I cannot thank you enough for your continued wisdom, especially Kim Hall, Sandy Sufian, Sue Schweik, and Rosemarie Garland Thomson. Sadly, we have also suffered profound losses: Anita Silvers, Paul Longmore, and Dan Wilson are deeply missed, and their work continues to influence and inspire my own. I am fortunate to have colleagues at Providence College who support my philosophical work, generously share their knowledge and friendship, and make teaching philosophy a pleasure. I shared early ideas of this project with colleagues as part of the Interdisciplinary Faculty Seminar. I was particularly lucky to be able to collaborate with my good friend Peter Costello on an edited book, *Phenomenology and the Arts*. It allowed my own ideas to take shape, and Peter's support was unwavering. A heartfelt thank you especially to Chris Arroyo, Emann Alleban, Antonella Mallozzi, Tim Mahoney, Jeff Nicholas, Vance Morgan, Laura Landen, Amy Almeida, my "Civ dream team" colleagues Stephanie Boeninger and Margaret Manchester, Tuba Agartan, Debby Levine, and Bill Hogan (my PC chamber music partner). Finally, I continue to learn so much from my wonderful students, whose curiosity, engagement, and diverse interests make my teaching life a pleasure and enrich my scholarly life in many unexpected ways.

I would not have written this book had it not been for so many who have shaped my musical life and have given me the gift of being part of a "musical we" over the years. Thank you to all of my music teachers, professors, fellow musicians, conductors, and my wonderful co-performers in the Longwood Symphony Orchestra, who model the true intersection between music and healing and who share their talents with me. I also want to honor the memory of two incredible chamber music coaches who gave me a deep love of ensemble playing: Luis Garcia Renart, cellist at Vassar College, and Vince Lionti, violist for the Met Orchestra, who both died of Covid last year. And to the brilliant luthier Sofia Vettori, who made my beautiful violin, named "Sospiri" after the bridge in Venice, thank you for giving me a second voice.

To my incredible group of friends (many of whom I have already mentioned), especially Jen, Kirsten, Lara, Corinne, Carola, Tania, Stefania, and the Arlington moms. You have patiently listened to my ideas and my music and provided me with support, laughter, your own brilliant music, wisdom, joy, and affection; you make my life so much sweeter. To Michael and my fellow philosopher-violinist Kathrin, thank you for sharing in my musical, philosophical, and personal worlds for all these years. And last but not least, I am so lucky to have such a beautiful, generous, musical family. Thank you to Murray and Joanna, who made me love jazz even more, and whom I miss immeasurably. To the Frank and Scarsella families, thank you for being my siblings and for enlarging and enriching my life. To my parents, thank you for taking me to lessons, for coming to my concerts, for always listening to my ideas, for carefully reading every word I have written, for taking such good care of my little family, and for lovingly making my world possible in every way. And to Jeremiah and Julian, who make me laugh, spoil me, share music with me, and have helped me get through this book and this pandemic unscathed, your love, humor, and gifts sustain me every day.

Notes

A Pandemic Preface

1. https://sevenlastwords.org.
2. Tom Huizenga, "Clarinetist Anthony McGill Kneels, Pleads and Plays for Justice," NPR, https://www.npr.org/sections/deceptivecadence/2020/06/04/868816095/clarinetist-anthony-mcgill-kneels-pleads-and-plays-for-justice.
3. Giulia Heyward, "Violin Vigils Honor the Memory of Elijah McClain," *New York Times*, July 13, 2020, https://www.nytimes.com/2020/07/13/arts/music/elijah-mccl ain-violin-vigil.html.
4. Licia Carlson and Sandy Sufian, "Thoughts on Precarity, Risk, and Disablement during COVID-19," in *The Boundaries of Disability: Critical Reflections*, ed. Licia Carlson and Matthew Murray (New York: Routledge, 2020), 124–37; Jonathan Gleason et al., "The Devastating Impact of Covid-19 on Individuals with Intellectual Disabilities in the United States," *NEJM Catalyst*, March 5, 2021, https://catalyst.nejm.org/doi/full/10.1056/CAT.21.0051; Ryan H. Nelson and Leslie Francis, "Intellectual Disability and Justice in a Pandemic," *Kennedy Institute of Ethics Journal*, special issue, https://kiej.georgetown.edu/intellectual-disability-pandemic-special-issue/; Ari Ne'eman, "I Will Not Apologize for My Needs," *New York Times*, March 23, 2020, https://www.nytimes.com/2020/03/23/opinion/coronavirus-ventilators-triage-disability.html?searchResultPosition=1.

Introduction

1. This idea in my book *The Faces of Intellectual Disability* was inspired by Georgina Kleege's claim that the blind are a filmmaker's worst nightmare. See "Introduction: The Philosopher's Nightmare," in Licia Carlson, *The Faces of Intellectual Disability: Philosophical Reflections* (Bloomington: Indiana University Press, 2009), 1–4.
2. Pianist and disability theorist Stefan Sunandan Honisch has written extensively on the reception of Tsujii's work from a disability studies perspective. He delves into the complex relationship between disability, normalcy, and virtuosity in Stefan Sunandan Honisch, "Virtuosities of Deafness and Blindness: Musical Performance and the Prized Body," in *The Oxford Handbook of Music and the Body*, ed. Youn Kim and Sander Gilman (New York: Oxford University Press, 2019), 276–94.

3. Northeast Music Cognition Group (NEMCOG), Harvard University, January 2016.
4. http://sonification.de/son/definition.
5. Psyche Loui, Matan Koplin-Green, Mark Frick, and Michael Massone, "Rapidly Learned Identification of Epileptic Seizures from Sonified EEG," *Frontiers in Human Neuroscience* 8 (2014): 1–9. https://doi.org/10.3389/fnhum.2014.00820.
6. Disability has affected my life in various ways through those around me, but I am a non-disabled (or "temporarily abled"), white, cisgendered philosophy professor who has benefited from the privileges that come with these identities. This includes my access to music and musical education, my degrees in music and philosophy, and the many ways in which I benefit from ableist, classist, and racist structural inequalities. To offer a musical analogy, when I speak about disability, I am a witness, committed to learning, engaging, and collaborating, but I do not pretend to know the full score.
7. Kathleen Marie Higgins, *The Music of Our Lives* (Lanham, MD: Lexington, 2011), 114. Alperson and Carroll echo this when they suggest that analytic philosophy of music has been too narrowly focused on "absolute music or music alone." See Philip Alperson and Noel Carroll, "Music, Mind, and Morality: Arousing the Body Politic," *Journal of Aesthetic Education* 42, no. 1 (Spring 2008): 3.
8. While a growing number of philosophers of disability are approaching disability from a broad range of perspectives (not just in ethics and political philosophy but also in philosophy of mind, epistemology, philosophy of science, feminist philosophy, and critical race theory), there is very little work that addresses aesthetic questions in relation to disability generally and intellectual disability specifically. There are a few exceptions, all of whom have greatly influenced how I approach music, philosophy, and disability together and have informed many of the arguments in this book; these include Anita Silvers, Eva Kittay, and John Vorhaus.
9. See Tobin Siebers, *Disability Aesthetics* (Ann Arbor: University of Michigan Press, 2010); Carrie Sandhal and Philip Auslander, eds., *Bodies in Commotion* (Ann Arbor: University of Michigan Press, 2005); Georgina Kleege, *More Than Meets the Eye: What Blindness Brings to Art* (New York: Oxford University Press, 2018); Blake Howe et al., eds., *The Oxford Handbook of Music and Disability Studies* (New York: Oxford University Press, 2015); Joseph Straus, *Extraordinary Measures: Disability in Music* (New York: Oxford University Press, 2011); Alex Lubet, *Music, Disability, and Society* (Philadelphia: Temple University Press, 2011); Neil Lerner and Joseph Straus, eds., *Sounding Off: Theorizing Disability in Music* (New York: Routledge, 2006); William Cheng, *Just Vibrations: The Purpose of Sounding Good* (Ann Arbor: University of Michigan, 2016); George McKay, *Shakin' All Over: Popular Music and Disability* (Ann Arbor: University of Michigan Press, 2013).
10. http://sonification.de/son/definition.
11. Alexandra Supper, "Sublime Frequencies: The Construction of Sublime Listening Experiences in the Sonification of Scientific Data," *Social Studies of Science* 44, no. 1 (2014): 34–58. In this article, Supper discusses the ways sonification has been used both in art and to popularize science.

12. Stephen Barrass, Michael Whitelaw, and Guillaume Potard, "Listening to the Mind Listening: Practice Based Research in EEG Sonification," *Media International Australia Incorporating Culture and Policy* 118, no. 1 (2006): 60, http://doi.org/10.1177/1329878X0611800109.
13. Elizabeth Gibney, "How One Astronomer Hears the Universe," *Nature* 577 (January 2020): 155. An example related to intellectual disability is the development of "biomusic," an interface that "maps physiological signals to music" to detect anxiety in children with profound intellectual disabilities. This raises a host of ethical and philosophical questions that I will not address here, but I mention it as another example of how sonification technology connects with disability. See Stephanie Cheung et al., "Biomusic: An Auditory Interface for Detecting Physiological Indicators of Anxiety in Children," *Frontiers of Neuroscience* 10 (2016): 401, https://doi.org/10.3389/fnins.2016.00401.
14. Gibney, "How One Astronomer Hears the Universe."
15. Christopher Small, *Musicking: The Meanings of Performing and Listening* (Middletown, CT: Wesleyan University Press, 1998), 8–9.
16. Rosemarie Garland Thomson, "Misfits: A Feminist Materialist Disability Concept," *Hypatia* 26, no. 3 (Summer 2011): 591–609, https://doi.org/10.1111/j.1527-2001.2011.01206.x. There are many debates and varied definitions of models of disability (e.g., social, postmodern, materialist) within disability studies.
17. Critical disability studies has emerged as a distinct approach to disability studies grounded in a number of political and theoretical commitments that I embrace, including intersectionality, cross-disability solidarity, interdependence, and collective access and liberation. See Patricia Berne et al., "Ten Principles of Disability Justice," *WSQ: Women's Studies Quarterly* 46, nos. 1–2 (Spring/Summer 2018): 227–30; Sami Schalk, "Coming to Claim Crip: Disidentification with/in Disability Studies," *Disability Studies Quarterly* 33, no. 2 (2013), https://doi.org/10.18061/dsq.v33i2.3705; Alison Kafer, *Feminist, Queer, Crip* (Bloomington: Indiana University Press, 2013).
18. There is vast terminological, etiological, and diagnostic landscape here, including a range of institutional discourses that define these categories and individuals. In using the term "intellectual disability," I will be referring primarily to the conditions that fall under the American Association on Intellectual and Developmental Disabilities' definition: "a disability characterized by significant limitations in both intellectual functioning and in adaptive behavior, which covers many everyday social and practical skills, with onset before the age of 22" (https://www.aaidd.org/intellectual-disability/definition). For additional discussions of the complexities of this terminology, see Carlson, *Faces*; Licia Carlson, "On Moral Status and Intellectual Disability: Challenging and Expanding the Debates," in *The Oxford Handbook of Philosophy and Disability*, ed. Adam Cureton and David Wasserman (New York: Oxford University Press, 2019), 482–97.
19. Rosemarie Garland Thomson, "The Case for Conserving Disability," *Journal of Bioethical Inquiry* 9 (September 2012): 339–55.
20. Susan McClary, *Feminine Endings: Music, Gender, and Sexuality* (Minneapolis: University of Minnesota Press, 1991).

21. For an overview of work on feminism and disability in philosophy, see Licia Carlson, "Feminism and Disability Theory," in *The Oxford Handbook of Feminist Philosophy*, ed. Kim Hall and Ásta Sveinsdóttir (New York: Oxford University Press, 2021), 516–30. See also Kim Hall, ed., *Feminist Disability Studies* (Bloomington: Indiana University Press, 2011); Shelley Tremain, ed., "Special Issue: Improving Feminist Philosophy and Theory by Taking Account of Disability," *Disability Studies Quarterly* 33, no. 4 (2013), https://doi.org/10.18061/dsq.v33i4; Rosemarie Garland Thomson, "Feminist Disability Studies," *Signs: Journal of Women in Culture and Society* 30, no. 2 (2005): 1557–87; Sami Schalk and Jina B. Kim, "Integrating Race, Transforming Feminist Disability Studies," *Signs: Journal of Women in Culture and Society* 46, no. 1 (2020): 31–55.
22. For example, there are traditions that define both the "musical work" and the "disabled body" in essentialist terms, and it is interesting to consider parallels between the critiques of these.
23. See Joseph Straus, "Idiots Savants, Retarded Savants, Talented Aments, Mono-Savants, Autistic Savants, Just Plain Savants, People with Savant Syndrome, and Autistic People Who Are Good at Things: A View from Disability Studies," *Disability Studies Quarterly* 34, no. 3 (2014), https://doi.org/10.18061/dsq.v34i3.3407; Straus, *Extraordinary Measures*; Howe et al., *Oxford Handbook*.
24. See Jeff Warren, *Music and Ethical Responsibility* (Cambridge: Cambridge University Press, 2014), 180–83; Cheng, *Just Vibrations*, 71–75.
25. Licia Carlson, "Encounters with Musical Others," in *Phenomenology and the Arts*, ed. Licia Carlson and Peter Costello (Lanham, MD: Lexington, 2015), 235–52.
26. Tia DeNora, *Music Asylums: Wellbeing through Music in Everyday Life* (Farnham, UK: Ashgate, 2013).
27. Peter Kivy, "Musical Morality," *Revue Internationale de Philosophie* 4 (2009): 397–412.
28. Nietzsche, Friedrich. *The Will to Power*. Translated by Walter Kaufmann, (New York: Vintage, 1967).
    Gabriel Marcel, *Music and Philosophy*, trans. Stephen Maddux and Robert E. Wood (Milwaukee: Marquette University Press, 2005); Jan Zwicky, *Lyric Philosophy* (Edmonton: Brusch Education, 2014); Ludwig Wittgenstein, *Culture and Value*, ed. G. H. Von Wright, trans. Peter Winch (Chicago: University of Chicago Press, 1980).
29. Alfred Schutz, "Making Music Together: A Study in Social Relationship," *Social Research* 18, no. 1 (1951): 76–97.

Chapter 1

1. I prefer the terms "witness" and "beholder" to "listener" or "audience member," as they capture a broader group of musical subjects. This includes those who do not "listen to" or "hear" music in traditional, aural means (e.g., deaf individuals) and

those who partake in musicking in settings that do not involve a formal structure of performance/audience.
2. Pablo Neruda, *All the Odes*, ed. Ilan Stavans (New York: Farrar, Straus and Giroux, 2013), 704.
3. Lydia Goehr presents a genealogy of the "musical work" in *The Imaginary Museum of Musical Works: An Essay in the Philosophy of Music* (Oxford: Oxford University Press, 2007).
4. Roman Ingarden, *Ontology of the Work of Art* (Athens: University of Ohio Press, 1998), 93.
5. Bruce Benson, *The Improvisation of Musical Dialogue: A Phenomenology of Music* (Cambridge: Cambridge University Press, 2003), 154.
6. Ingarden, *Ontology*, 115.
7. Mikel Dufrenne, *The Phenomenology of Aesthetic Experience* (Evanston, IL: Northeastern University Press, 1973), 251.
8. Pianist Alfred Brendel writes, "To understand the composer's intentions means to translate them into one's own understanding. Music cannot 'speak for itself.'" Quoted in John Rink, "Impersonating the Music in Performance," in *The Oxford Handbook of Musical Identities*, ed. Raymond Macdonald, David J. Hargreaves, and Dorothy Miell (New York: Oxford University Press, 2017), 359.
9. Benson, *Improvisation*, 154–55.
10. Joseph Straus, *Broken Beauty: Musical Modernism and the Representation of Disability* (Oxford: Oxford University Press, 2018), 39.
11. Alfred Schutz, "Making Music Together: A Study in Social Relationship," *Social Research* 18, no. 1 (1951): 90.
12. Michel Foucault, "What Is an Author?," in *Michel Foucault: Aesthetics, Method and Epistemology*, ed. James D. Faubion (New York: New Press, 1998), 205.

Chapter 2

1. Jerrold Levinson, *Musical Concerns: Essays in Philosophy of Music* (Oxford: Oxford University Press, 2015), 81.
2. Higgins, *Music of Our Lives*, 120.
3. The question of how to define the "self" is complex and has a long philosophical history. For the purposes of my discussion here, I view a self as an individual who is embodied and who possesses some degree of awareness, self-consciousness, and agency (though this can vary tremendously and is not always easily verifiable). Rather than a static or fixed entity, the self is dynamic, performative, and capable of transformation over time. Finally, a self always exists in relation to others and is thus interdependent and has an identity that can be shaped by both external and internal factors.
4. For an in-depth account of musical subjectivity for the performer, see Naomi Cummings, *The Sonic Self* (Bloomington: Indiana University Press, 2000). For a broad range of discussions related to "musical identities" within the field of music

psychology, see Raymond Macdonald, David J. Hargreaves, and Dorothy Miell, eds., *The Oxford Handbook of Musical Identities* (New York: Oxford University Press, 2017).
5. For various perspectives on music and embodiment, see Youn Kim and Sander L. Gilman, eds., *The Oxford Handbook of Music and the Body* (New York: Oxford University Press, 2019).
6. Cummings, *Sonic Self*, 12–13.
7. Vijay Iyer, "On Improvisation, Temporality, and Embodied Experience," in *Sound Unbound: Sampling Digital Music and Culture*, ed. Paul D. Miller (Cambridge: MIT Press, 2008), 287.
8. Vijay Iyer, "Exploding the Narrative in Jazz Improvisation," in *Uptown Conversations: The New Jazz Studies*, ed. Robert O'Meally, Brent Hayes Edwards, and Farah Jasmine Griffin (New York: Columbia University Press, 2004), 402.
9. See Jerrold Levinson and Philip Alperson, "What Is a Temporal Art?," in Levinson, *Musical Concerns*, 162. Iyer, too, talks about the temporality of musical encounters.
10. Quoted in Levinson and Alperson, "What Is a Temporal Art?," 162.
11. The discussion that follows is drawn from Carlson, "Encounters."
12. Edmund Husserl, *The Phenomenology of Internal Time-Consciousness*, ed. Martin Heidegger, trans. James Churchill (Bloomington: Indiana University Press, 1964). Husserl calls these two modes of perception protention and retention.
13. Schutz, "Making Music Together," 88.
14. Schutz, "Making Music Together," 89.
15. I am grateful to Stephen Unwin for making this point.
16. Musicologist and pianist John Rink discusses the difficulty of articulating and defining the "musical feeling" that a musician experiences when performing: "informally, it may be described as a 'gut feeling,' whereby the music's motion and trajectory are inscribed deep within." Rink, "Impersonating," 351.
17. Warren, *Music and Ethical Responsibility*, 162.
18. Benson, *Improvisation*, 179.
19. Kathleen Higgins, *The Music between Us: Is Music a Universal Language?* (University of Chicago Press, 2014), 162.
20. Higgins, *Music between Us*, 163.
21. Of course, other arts are contingent and finite as well, and it is worth exploring further how the nature of permanence and contingency in music compares to that in other forms.
22. Garry Hagberg, "Jazz Improvisation and Ethical Interaction: A Sketch of the Connections," in *Art and Ethical Criticism*, ed. Garry Hagberg (Malden, MA: Blackwell, 2008), 270.
23. I focus on musical joy here because it is related to elements of the shared musical experience and dimensions of flourishing that I will address later. But there is a much larger discussion and debate regarding the relationship between emotions and music. For a good overview of philosophical theories of music and the emotions, see Jennifer Robinson, *Deeper Than Reason: Emotion and Its Role in Literature, Music, and Art* (New York: Oxford University Press, 2005), especially chapters 10–13. For a discussion of musical catharsis in blues music, see Roopen Majithia, "Blues and Catharsis," in

Blues Philosophy for Everyone: Thinking Deep about Feeling Low, ed. Jesse R. Steinberg and Abrol Fairweather (Malden, MA: Wiley-Blackwell, 2012), 84–93.
24. Higgins, *Music of Our Lives*, 120.
25. In the classical realm, Beethoven and Smetana come to mind, for example; in the context of disability, there is a range of work by composers and performers who are at once challenging forms of ableism and creatively expanding the nature of performance. For example, see Molly Joyce (mollyjoyce.com); sinsinvalid.org; Leroy Moore's Krip-Hop Nation (kriphopnation.com).
26. There is an entire body of philosophical and musical literature about what constitutes an *authentic* performance. See, for example, Richard Taruskin, *Text and Act: Essays on Musical Performance* (Oxford: Oxford University Press, 1995).
27. I will say more about this in chapters 3 and 5.
28. DeNora, *Music Asylums*.
29. Marcel, *Music and Philosophy*, 137.
30. Oliver Sacks, *Musicophilia: Tales of Music and the Brain* (New York: Vintage, 2008), chapter 29. There is a broad range of studies in the field of music therapy that confirm the effects of music on these populations. For powerful examples of the effects of music on individuals with dementia, see the film *Alive Inside: A Story of Music and Memory* (www.aliveinside.us). For many additional examples of this in the context of music therapy, see Gary Ansdell, *How Music Helps in Music Therapy and Everyday Life* (New York: Routledge, 2015).
31. Sacks, *Musicophilia*, 346. Sacks's examples in *Musicophilia* and in his other books introduce many important questions and profile a variety of conditions and individual experiences. At the same time, disability theorists have been wary of a predominantly medicalized or pathologized approach that some see in his work. See Simi Linton, "Disability Studies, Not Disability Studies," *Disability and Society* 13, no. 4 (1998): 525–40; Leonard Cassuto, "Oliver Sacks: The P. T. Barnum of the Postmodern World?," *American Quarterly* 53, no. 2 (June 2000): 326–33. On *Musicophilia* in relation to disability studies specifically, see Leonard Cassuto, "The Uncanny Symphony of Oliver Sacks," *Chronicle of Higher Education*, November 2, 2007, https://www.chronicle.com/article/the-uncanny-symphony-of-oliver-sacks/?cid2=gen_lo gin_refresh&cid=gen_sign_in.
32. DeNora, *Music Asylums*, 1.
33. Examples that cut across genres of music include protest music and pieces that express the horrors of war (e.g., Penderecki's *Threnody to the Victims of Hiroshima*), requiem masses and other forms of music to honor the dead, and musical responses to misogyny and racial oppression and violence. In the context of disability and police brutality, for example, Krip-Hop Nation released the CD *Broken Bodies, PBP Police Brutality Profiling Mixtape* in 2012.
34. See Frederick Douglass, *Narrative of the Life of Frederick Douglass* (London: Penguin Classics, 2016); Angela Davis, *Blues Legacies and Black Feminism* (New York: Vintage, 1998).
35. Cornel West, "Black Strivings in a Twilight Civilization," in Cornel West, *The Cornel West Reader* (New York: Basic Civitas, 1999), 100. For a philosophical discussion

of these themes in blues music, see Jesse R. Steinberg and Abrol Fairweather, eds., *Blues Philosophy for Everyone: Thinking Deep about Feeling Low* (Malden, MA: Wiley-Blackwell, 2012).
36. Alperson and Carroll speak about many examples like these in "Music, Mind, and Morality."
37. M. J. Grant makes this point in "The Illogical Logic of Music Torture," *Torture* 23, no. 2 (2013): 4–13. For an example of the redemptive effects of music during the Holocaust, see the powerful film *They Played for Their Lives* (theyplayedfortheirlives.com). As one survivor, Alice, tells it, "They tore off our belongings, food and clothing but music is the one thing that they could not take away from us, music that evil could not destroy." For other discussions of sonic warfare, see Warren, *Music and Ethical Responsibility*, 180–83; Cheng, *Just Vibrations*, chapter 4.
38. There is a robust body of work on music and disability within the interdisciplinary field of disability studies that addresses these question from many different angles. See Howe et al., *The Oxford Handbook of Music and Disability Studies*; Straus, *Extraordinary Measures*; Lubet, *Music Disability*; Lerner and Straus, *Sounding Off*.
39. Sandahl and Auslander, *Bodies in Commotion*, 10.
40. Blake Howe, "Disabling Music Performance," in *The Oxford Handbook of Music and Disability Studies*, ed. Blake Howe, Stephanie Jensen-Moulton, Neil Lerner, and Joseph Straus (New York: Oxford University Press, 2015), 191 (quoting Joseph Straus).
41. Stefan Sunandan Honisch, "'Re-narrating Disability' through Musical Performance," *Music Theory Online* 15, nos. 3–4 (August 2009), https://mtosmt.org/issues/mto.09.15.3/mto.09.15.3.honisch.html.
42. Howe, "Disabling Music Performance," 198, 200.
43. Howe, "Disabling Music Performance," 202.
44. https://paraorchestra.com/about/.
45. Lubet, *Music, Disability, and Society*, 42. He goes on to analyze the impact of injury and disability on Django Reinhardt, Horace Parlan, and Jimmy Scott; see 42–68.
46. Quoted in Colin Hambrook, "Interview: Molly Joyce on the Influence of Disability Studies on Her Music-Making," *Disability Arts Online*, June 1, 2019, https://disabilityarts.online/magazine/opinion/molly-joyce/.
47. Evelyn Glennie, Sander L. Gilman, and Youn Kim, "Is There Disabled Music? Music and the Body from Dame Evelyn Glennie's Perspective," in *The Oxford Handbook of Music and the Body*, ed. Youn Kim and Sander L. Gilman (New York: Oxford University Press, 2019), 324.
48. See the documentary by directors Margie Friedman and Barbara Multer-Wellin, *Orchestrating Change*, PBS, 2021, https://orchestratingchangethefilm.com.
49. Michael Watts and Barbara Ridley, "Identities of Dis/ability and Music," *British Educational Research Journal* 38, no. 3 (2012): 366. It is important to note that the term "learning disability" in the United Kingdom corresponds to the category "intellectual and developmental disability" in the United States.
50. Grace explains that she is "alexithymic," which means having "difficulty in understanding and ascribing affective labels to one's own physiological states of arousal."

This definition is quoted by Bakan, though Grace challenges the assumption that this condition means that "alexithymic types don't actually have feelings." See "Elizabeth J. 'Ibby' Grace," in Michael Bakan, *Music and Autism: Speaking for Ourselves* (New York: Oxford University Press, 2018), 75. The diversity of perspectives in the chapters of Bakan's book attests to the range of ways in which music can provide a "sonic identity" for autistic persons.

51. CD notes, *Music of Hikari Oe*, Vol. 1, Denon CO-78952, 1994.
52. See Licia Carlson, "Musical Becoming: Intellectual Disability and the Transformative Power of Music," in *Foundations of Disability Studies*, ed. Matthew Wappett and Katrina Arndt (London: Palgrave Macmillan, 2013), 83–103.
53. Straus, *Extraordinary Measures*, 43.
54. Sacks, *Musicophilia*, 328. Though he clarifies that many people with Williams syndrome are not musical savants, when Sacks refers to their "extraordinary constellation of cognitive talents and deficits" and defines them as a "hypermusical *species*," there is danger of further othering them.
55. For a discussion of musical ability in individuals with Williams syndrome, see Daniel Levitin and Ursula Belugi, "Musical Abilities in Individuals with Williams Syndrome," *Music Perception* 15, no. 4 (1998): 357–89; Howard M. Lenhoff, Olegario Perales, and Gregory Hickok, "Absolute Pitch in Williams Syndrome," *Music Perception* 18, no. 4 (2001): 491–503. While these scientific studies confirm facets of musical capacities that are significant, there are also elements of studying this group as research subjects that are important to critically address and problematize. For the story of Gloria Lenhoff, see Terry Sforza with Howard and Sylvia Lenhoff, *The Strangest Song: One Father's Quest to Help His Daughter Find Her Voice* (Amherst, NY: Prometheus, 2006).
56. John Vorhaus and Adam Ockelford, "Identity and Musical Development in People with Severe or Profound and Multiple Learning Disabilities," in *The Oxford Handbook of Musical Identities*, ed. Raymond Macdonald, David J. Hargreaves, and Dorothy Miell (New York: Oxford University Press, 2017), 642–67. The research here is based on the "Sounds of Intent" project that was intended to "map the musical development of children and young people with learning difficulties" (643). One case study is of Sandip, age eleven, who has "severe learning disabilities, visual processing difficulties, and a diagnosis of autism": "Sandip has acquired a significant (though presumably non-linguistic) form of narrative self, since he can understand how series of notes presented over time can form groups, and how these can be used to create more substantial sequences that he can formulate on his own or by participating with others.... Hence, Sandip is giving evidence of having an awareness of self that includes a developing sense of self-consciousness, a sense of a continuing self enduring over time, and a self that is able to interact with and respond to the non-linguistic communicative and other behaviors of his teacher and parents" (661–62).
57. Vorhaus and Ockelford, "Identity," 665. See Ansdell, *How Music Helps*, for numerous other examples.
58. It is important to stress that there are many other forms of nonverbal communication that are effective and that allow forms of self-expression: signs, gestures, body language, assistive devices. Music is just one possibility among many.

59. Though this term has been almost universally retired and has been extensively critiqued by disability scholars (myself included), it still appears occasionally in some scientific and medical literature associated with various forms of intellectual and developmental disabilities. See Carlson, *Faces*.
60. www.danielsmusic.org.
61. See Jerome Preisler with the Trush family, *Daniel's Music: One Family's Journey from Tragedy to Empowerment through Faith, Medicine, and the Healing Power of Music* (New York: Skyhorse, 2015).
62. DeNora, *Music Asylums*, 1.

Chapter 3

1. For discussions of music in Plato and Aristotle, see Eva Brann, *The Music of the Republic* (Philadelphia: Paul Dry, 2004); Göran Sörbom, "Aristotle on Music as Representation," in *Musical Worlds: New Directions in the Philosophy of Music*, ed. Philip Alperson (University Park: Pennsylvania State University Press, 1998), 37–46. Of course, between the Greeks and contemporary philosophers of music, there are a plethora of philosophers who have addressed music. A few who come to mind include Boethius, Saint Augustine, Rousseau, Schopenhauer, Nietzsche, Adorno, Marcel, Wittgenstein, and Deleuze.
2. Kivy cites examples of Germans playing and using music in Auschwitz, one of the most powerful and dehumanizing abuses of music. In *Survival in Auschwitz*, Primo Levi describes the "infernal" music of the camps, the "dance of dead men": "The tunes are few, a dozen, the same ones every day, morning and evening: marches and popular songs dear to every German. They lie engraven on our minds and will be the last thing in the Lager that we shall forget: they are the voice of the Lager, the perceptible expression of its geometrical madness, of the resolution of others to annihilate us first as men in order to kill us later." Primo Levi, *Survival in Auschwitz*, trans. Stuart Woolf (New York: Simon & Schuster, 1995), 51. For other discussions of music as "sonic warfare," see note 37 in chapter 2.
3. Kivy, "Musical Morality," 398.
4. Kivy, "Musical Morality," 398. Though I will not wade into these arguments here, I am inclined to agree with Kivy on this point regarding absolute music. However, I also agree with the point Alperson and Carroll make regarding the problematic notion of speaking about "music alone." They claim that while the skeptic will rightly argue that absolute music, or "*music alone*," cannot have any moral or epistemic meaning by virtue of its being free of any semantic content, most music is not, in fact, *music alone*; they go on to emphasize that "most music has not been absolute music. Historically (and cross-culturally), music evolved in tandem with song, epic poetry, dance, ritual, and drama.... Whether or not absolute music has the kind of semantic machinery it takes to transmit religious, moral, political, spiritual, and otherwise cultural messages and sentiments, song, epic poetry, ritual, dance, and drama have those capabilities.

Music, accompanied collectively or distributively with the aforesaid referential practices, does have the power to do the things that the skeptic denies that music alone can achieve." Alperson and Carroll, "Music, Mind, and Morality," 3–4.
5. Jean-Jacques Rousseau, *Essay on the Origin of Languages and Writings Related to Music*, trans. John T. Scott (Hanover, NH: Dartmouth College Press, 1998), 138–9.
6. Of course, one could argue that singing is not a uniquely human endeavor, and I do not want to defend an exclusionary argument that views song as exclusively human. Birds and other animals produce forms of song, and the significance of this raises fascinating questions about animal cognition and behavior. However, I am deliberately focusing my discussion here on the production of music by and for human beings.
7. It is interesting to note that today, even in recorded music where the body is invisible, there is the presence of others—at the very least, the composer and performer, who may or may not be the same. One could argue that entirely computer-generated music, disembodied and without author or performer, would be an exception to this, though even this bears the mark of human programmers.
8. Vijay Iyer, "The Myth of the Solitary Listener: Music Cognition and the Humanities," unpublished keynote address delivered at the annual meeting of New England Music Cognition Group, Harvard University, 2016.
9. Higgins, *Music of Our Lives*, 128.
10. Levinson, *Musical Concerns*, 82; emphasis added.
11. Daniel Barenboim and Edward W. Said, *Parallels and Paradoxes: Explorations in Music and Society* (New York: Pantheon, 2002), 9.
12. Barenboim and Said, *Parallels*, 10.
13. I will address some of the problems with this notion later in the chapter.
14. Carlson, *Faces*; Carlson, "On Moral Status"; Eva Kittay and Licia Carlson, eds., *Cognitive Disability and Its Challenge to Moral Philosophy* (Malden, MA: Wiley-Blackwell, 2010); James Trent, *Inventing the Feeble Mind: A History of Intellectual Disability in the United States* (Oxford: Oxford University Press, 2016).
15. Vorhaus and Ockelford, "Identity." See also Ansdell, *How Music Helps*.
16. CD notes, *Music of Hikari Oe*. For more about Hikari Oe, see Lindsay Cameron, *The Music of Light: The Extraordinary Story of Kenzaburo and Hikari Oe* (New York: Free Press, 1998).
17. See Licia Carlson, "Music, Intellectual Disability, and Human Flourishing," in *The Oxford Handbook of Music and Disability Studies*, ed. Blake Howe et al. (New York: Oxford University Press, 2015), 42.
18. Levinson, *Musical Concerns*, 82.
19. I do not mean to suggest here that intellectually disabled people respond only to music without text. And it is interesting to consider to what extent it is the combination of lyrics and music that is the source of enjoyment.
20. Meryl Alper, *Giving Voice: Mobile Communication, Disability, and Inequality* (Cambridge, MA: MIT Press, 2017), 2. The subjects of Alper's study are all children with communicative impairments caused by a developmental disability encompassing a range of conditions, including autism, intellectual disabilities, and cerebral palsy (173). "Voicelessness," however, is a contentious issue, as many self-advocates have

pointed out that they may choose *not* to speak or that they are voiceless only in the sense that no one chooses to listen to them.

21. Alper, *Giving Voice*, 114.
22. Alper, *Giving Voice*, 112.
23. Alper, *Giving Voice*, 112–13.
24. Jeffrey Kittay, "The Sound Surround: Exploring How One Might Design the Everyday Soundscape for the Truly Captive Audience," *Nordic Journal of Music Therapy* 17, no. 1 (2008)): 41–54. See also Carlson, "Musical Becoming."
25. John Vorhaus, *Giving Voice to Profound Disability: Dignity, Dependence and Human Capabilities* (London: Routledge, 2016), 18–19.
26. Vorhaus, *Giving Voice*, 18–19.
27. I discuss and argue against certain "prototype effects" in Carlson, *Faces*, 165–77.
28. Of course, this is by no means simply relegated to music as an art form. There are myriad examples from across the art world, including dance, visual arts, multimedia, and theater. The sculptures of Judith Scott, for example, are a striking testament to the power of artistic production as representations of oneself and one's human experience. See John M. MacGregor, *Metamorphosis: The Fiber Art of Judith Scott* (Oakland, CA: Creative Growth Art Center, 1999). And it is worthy of further exploration to determine in what ways music, or these forms of *sonification*, differ from the knowledge that experiences of other arts yield.
29. See Carlson, *Faces*.
30. Carlson, *Faces*, 189–95.
31. For examples, both historical and contemporary, that engage with various forms of disabilities, see Howe et al., *Oxford Handbook*; Straus, *Extraordinary Measures*; Lubet, *Music, Disability, and Society*; Lerner and Straus, *Sounding Off*; McKay, *Shakin' All Over*.
32. In *Extraordinary Measures*, Straus gives examples of multiple kinds of hearing, including disablist and autistic.
33. Moreover, as I have already addressed, there are many examples of musical expression by individuals who would not qualify as "intelligent" according to certain metrics and would certainly have been excluded by Rousseau in his discussion of music. This statement also raises the question of whether there is a distinct form of "musical intelligence," defined most notably in Howard Gardner, *Intelligence Reframed: Multiple Intelligences for the 21st Century* (New York: Basic Books, 2000). Without wading into this much larger conversation, I will simply say here that I would not want to restrict meaningful musical experience solely to those who possess what is defined as "musical intelligence."
34. For a discussion of the role of women and gender in Rousseau's philosophy, see Lynda Lange, ed., *Feminist Interpretations of Jean-Jacques Rousseau* (University Park: Pennsylvania State University Press, 2002). For a discussion of Rousseau's theories of music and race, see the editors' introduction in Ronald M. Radano and Phillip V. Bohlman, eds., *Music and the Racial Imagination* (Chicago: University of Chicago Press, 2001), 15–18. They claim that for Rousseau, "through song, the racial difference immanent in nature was given voice" (18).

35. Howe, "Disabling Music Performance," 195.
36. The chapters in Blake et al., *Oxford Handbook*, offer an array of examples.
37. Straus, "Idiots Savants."
38. Straus, "Idiots Savants."
39. Straus, "Idiots Savants."
40. Susan Wendell, *The Rejected Body: Feminist Philosophical Reflections on Disability* (New York: Routledge, 1996), 64.
41. West, "Black Strivings in a Twilight Civilization," 100.
42. Leroy F. Moore Jr., Tiny aka Lisa Gray-Garcia, and Emmitt H. Thrower, "Black & Blue: Policing Disability & Poverty beyond Occupy," in *Occupying Disability: Critical Approaches to Community, Justice, and Decolonizing Disability*, ed. Pamela Block et al. (New York: Springer, 2016), 310.
43. See Carlson, *Faces*, chapter 4.
44. Higgins, *Music between Us*, 12. Of course, it is important to note the complex ways in which cultural differences mediate and shape musical encounters and our experience of music itself.
45. Siebers, *Disability Aesthetics*, 19.
46. Straus, *Extraordinary Measures*, 160.
47. Straus, *Extraordinary Measures*, 161. He characterizes the autistic listener as "someone who attends to the discrete musical event in all of its concrete detail (local coherence); who prefers the part to the whole; who is adept at creating associative networks (often involving private or idiosyncratic meanings); and who may have absolute pitch and a prodigious rote memory . . . [and] people with autism sometimes respond to music with their own vocalizations" (165).
48. Straus, *Extraordinary Measures*, 180. Straus recognizes the danger inherent in this project: that it risks reinscribing and reinforcing "the boundary between normal and disabled bodies." Yet he maintains that we cannot begin to dismantle the artificial boundary, the "wall" between "normal" and "disablist" hearing, "until we can define better what lies on either side of it" (180). Despite this resistance to essentializing "the disabled" and "disability," some have raised questions as to whether his definitions may reiterate certain problematic moves. In a response to Straus's book, George Tsiris writes, "I wonder whether the conceptualization of these 'disablist hearings' can run the potential danger of creating a new series of 'labels,' of which there are already plenty within the field of disability." Giorgos Tsiris, "Voices from the 'Ghetto': Music Therapy Perspectives on Disability and Music (A Response to Joseph Straus's Book *Extraordinary Measures: Disability in Music*)," *International Journal of Community Music* 6 (2013): 336.
49. "Elizabeth J. 'Ibby' Grace," in Bakan, *Music and Autism*, 69–92.
50. See http://www.friendshipcircle.org/blog/2013/03/08/5-amazing-bands-who-look-beyond-their-disabilities/; https://www.interplayorchestra.org. The website for the band Flame describes it as "a group of musicians with powerful vocals, smooth harmonies and a rich array of instruments, the 10-person cover band from Gloversville, NY happens to have disabilities. The musicians of Flame have disabilities including autism, Down syndrome, cerebral palsy, blindness and paralysis, but that doesn't hold

them back. They do what they love and change the world along the way." http://www.flametheband.com.
51. Giles Perring, "The Facilitation of Learning-Disabled Arts: A Cultural Perspective," in *Bodies in Commotion: Disability and Performance*, ed. Carrie Sandahl and Philip Auslander (Ann Arbor: University of Michigan Press, 2005), 175.
52. Perring, "Facilitation," 187.
53. In his ethnographic study of artists involved in these programs, Perring identifies three methodological approaches: normalizing (focused on bringing people with learning disabilities into mainstream performance discourse), post-therapeutic (informed by therapeutic standpoints, this approach aims at allowing the person's "issues" to be expressed), and countercultural (an "objective that challenges mainstream cultural and aesthetic precepts and views about disability"). Perring argues that there are differences between a normalizing and a countercultural approach that "mirror the dialectic between integration and inclusion," whereby the former says, "Bring people inside the existing margins!" and the latter says, "Move the margins out so that everyone is inside them!" Perring, "Facilitation," 186.
54. Perring, "Facilitation," 186.
55. Perring, "Facilitation," 186.
56. Perring, "Facilitation," 185.
57. Many of the questions regarding epistemic and moral authority that I discuss in my article "Who's the Expert?" are applicable here as well. See Licia Carlson, "Who's the Expert? Rethinking Authority in Light of Intellectual Disability," *Journal of Intellectual Disability Research* 54, supp. 1 (March 2010): 58–65.

Chapter 4

1. Jan Zwicky, "What Is Lyric Philosophy? An Introduction," *Common Knowledge* 20, no. 1 (Winter 2014): 16.
2. Jan Zwicky, *Lyric Philosophy* (Edmonton: Brush Education, 2014), §302.
3. The concept of "disability gain" and "deaf gain" are important ones in disability theory. They capture the idea that disability and deafness are experiences that are generative and positive and that yield specific knowledge and contributions.
4. Eva Kittay, *Learning from My Daughter: The Value and Care of Disabled Minds* (Oxford: Oxford University Press, 2019), 249.
5. Friedrich Nietzsche, *The Will to Power*, trans. Walter Kaufmann (New York: Vintage, 1967), 810.
6. Zwicky, "What Is Lyric Philosophy?" 19.
7. Zwicky, *Lyric Philosophy*, §251.
8. Zwicky, *Lyric Philosophy*, §132.
9. Stephen Unwin, "The Sound of Silence: My Joey Does Not Need to Speak to Be Heard," *Byline Times*, September 18, 2021. https://bylinetimes.com/2021/09/17/the-sound-of-silence-my-joey-doesnt-need-to-speak-to-be-heard/

10. This is taken from an interview with Scottish percussionist Dame Evelyn Glennie, who is deaf. Glennie, Gilman, and Kim, "Is There Disabled Music?," 327. Glennie is also the subject of a powerful documentary *Touch the Sound*.
11. Nancy Mairs, *Waist-High in the World: A Life among the Nondisabled* (Boston: Beacon, 1996), 63.
12. Maria Lugones, "Playfulness, World-Travelling, and Loving Perception," in *Feminist Social Thought: A Reader*, ed. Diana Tietjens Meyer (New York: Routledge, 1989), 158.
13. Lugones, "Playfulness."
14. Friedrich Nietzsche, *The Dionysian Vision of the World*, trans. Ira J. Allen (Minneapolis: Univocal, 2013), 51.
15. Ludwig Wittgenstein, *Culture and Value*, ed. G. H. Von Wright, trans. Peter Winch (Chicago: University of Chicago Press, 1980), 73e.
16. I borrow this term from Margaret Price, "The Bodymind Problem and the Possibilities of Pain," *Hypatia* 30, no. 1 (2014): 268–84.
17. Gabriel Marcel, *Being and Having*, trans. Katharine Farrer (Westminster, UK: Dacre, 1949), 117.

Chapter 5

1. Zwicky, "What Is Lyric Philosophy?," 25.
2. Warren, *Music and Ethical Responsibility*, 163.
3. Schutz, "Making Music Together," 94–95. Similar dynamics can be found in other art forms such as theater and dance as well.
4. Schutz, "Making Music Together," 92.
5. Both Bruce Benson and Jeff Warren speak about music as a gift. See Benson, *Improvisation*, 187–88; Warren, *Music and Ethical Responsibility*, 169–70.
6. Davis, *Blues Legacies*. This kind of reciprocal participation in musicking can be found in many places past and present, including in churches and other venues where music has been made available to a wider audience.
7. Gary Ansdell elaborates on ideas of musical time and space and presents many compelling examples. Ansdell, *How Music Helps*. Philip Alperson writes: "Objects of the art form require time in presentation, that is, they require performance or exposition of some sort over an interval of time; the parts of the artwork are not all available at any one moment, but only consecutively." Alperson explains that this is true not only of music but also of "dance, film, kinetic sculpture, spoken poetry" and that its temporal nature has historical significance: "There is also a historically important line of expression theorists extending from Schopenhauer and Hegel through Susanne Langer, each of whom places one art—music—at a strategic point in his or her theory on the basis of a specific temporal feature of music. The reason for this is that they have been convinced by the Kantian claim that time, as the form of inner sense, is intimately bound up with the very idea of consciousness and they believe that music

has an unusually strong referential relationship to time or time-consciousness." In Levinson and Alperson, "What Is a Temporal Art?," 168.
8. Higgins, *Music between Us*, 158–59.
9. Licia Carlson, "Music, Intellectual Disability, and Human Flourishing," in *The Oxford Handbook of Music and Disability Studies*, ed. Howe et al. (New York: Oxford University Press, 2015), 37–53.
10. Warren, *Music and Ethical Responsibility*, 163.
11. It is interesting to consider the place of art and music in the history of institutions for the intellectually disabled. For example, Langdon Down (after whom Down syndrome is named) constructed a theater/concert hall as part of the Normansfield Hospital built in 1868.
12. Kittay, "Sound Surround," 41–54.
13. It is important to note here that "music therapy" encompasses a broad range of practices and philosophies, and there are some approaches to music therapy that explicitly claim to eschew a normalizing approach. See, for example, Mercedes Pavlicevic, Gary Ansdell, and Even Ruud, eds., *Community Music Therapy* (London: Jessica Kingsley, 2014).
14. DeNora, *Music Asylums*.
15. See Preisler, *Daniel's Music*; www.danielsmusic.org.
16. In *The Music between Us*, Higgins defines "vitality effects" as "dynamic kinetic qualities of feeling that distinguish animate from inanimate" (152) and "are the means by which we gain a sense of being 'with' another person at any stage of life" (153).
17. Higgins, *Music between Us*, 150.
18. Of course, access to musicking is not always universal, and many of these same barriers can exist in a musical context as well. It is also important to acknowledge that musical encounters have the potential to be alienating and that musical spaces and performances can be experienced as negative, a point to which I will return at the end of the chapter.
19. Kittay, *Learning from My Daughter*, 121–22.
20. Some have viewed this kind of enjoyment as problematic and less valuable. Eduard Hanslick, for example, said the purely hedonic experiences of music are "pathological." See Eduard Hanslick, *On the Musically Beautiful*, trans. Geoffrey Payzant, (Indianapolis, IL: Hackett Publishing, 1986), 60.
21. Ansdell, *How Music Helps*, 55.
22. Ansdell, *How Music Helps*, 153.
23. In *Learning from My Daughter*, Kittay argues that a person is flourishing when "the person has (or has access to or can strive to attain, either on her own or assisted by another) the things an individual truly cares about" but also recognizes that "the possibility of disability can make the possibility of flourishing more precarious" (129). She goes on to say that objective lists of criteria may capture what many people require but are not necessarily capacious enough to encompass modes of flourishing for all individuals. She also clarifies that she uses the term "flourishing" to mean having a flourishing life across one's life span and one that includes "having a sense that we are flourishing, that we are living the life we want to live" (129, 191, 198).

24. Ansdell offers a rich array of examples of this in his book and even addresses the fact that the asymmetry between therapist and client can shift and often recede. Though there is still the professional context in which these musical encounters occur, his community approach to music therapy constitutes a departure from approaches to the therapeutic relationship grounded more explicitly in a medicalized model.
25. Vorhaus, *Giving Voice*, 80–81.
26. Michael Bakan speaks about the participation of individuals with autism in the ARTISM ensemble (which includes improvisatory techniques and diverse musical instruments played by autistic and non-autistic people) in this way: "musical projects like ARTISM hold the capacity to contribute productively and meaningfully to the causes of autistic self-advocacy and quality of life, modeling new horizons of possibility for the cultivation of neurodiverse environments of cultural co-creation and self-determination while transforming public perceptions of autism from the customary tropes of deficit, disorder, despair, hopelessness, to alternate visions of wholeness, ability, diversity, possibility, and acceptance." Michael Bakan, "Toward an Ethnographic Model of Disability in the Ethnomusicology of Autism," in *The Oxford Handbook of Music and Disability Studies*, ed. Blake Howe et al. (New York: Oxford University Press, 2015), 15–36. For another example, see the discussion of the Drake Music Project in Watts and Ridley, "Identities of Dis/ability and Music."
27. Carlson, "Musical Becoming."
28. Ralph Harper, *On Presence: Variations and Reflections* (Philadelphia: Trinity Press International, 1991), 6–7.
29. Harper, *On Presence*, 125.
30. Harper, *On Presence*, 17.
31. Harper, *On Presence*, 17.
32. I address Levinas's arguments more fully in Carlson, "Encounters with Musical Others."
33. EuroArtsChannel, "Conversation between Daniel Barenboim and Edward Said" 35:42, Aug. 15, 2014 https://www.youtube.com/watch?v=HWQCy6_TU3A
34. Jane O'Dea argues that "music in performance" is a species of moral education. It fosters the acquisition and exercise of certain morally relevant and desirable character traits and dispositions. Moreover, it accomplishes this through being itself a form of moral conduct, where one learns through doing and thereafter comes to love and to be capable of "practical wisdom." See Jane O'Dea, "Virtue in Musical Performance," *Journal of Aesthetic Education* 27, no. 1 (Spring 1993): 61. While O'Dea focuses on performance, I think it is interesting to consider how being a witness of the musical performance and enjoying it with others may be equally morally instructive and transformative.
35. There are numerous other works that address musical virtues. For example, see O'Dea, "Virtue"; Hagberg, "Jazz Improvisation."
36. Higgins, *Music of Our Lives*, 129. Of course, this is not always the case (consider nationalistic music and the role of martial music in wars).
37. Iyer, "The Myth of the Solitary Listener." Iyer discusses how work on music and embodied cognition, and recent research on mirror neurons, may contribute to our

understanding of empathy through music. Though he is not speaking about empathy as a *virtue*, research on this kind of musical connection provides an interesting opportunity for an interdisciplinary discussion of the nature of empathy in music. See Vijay Iyer, "Improvisation, Action Understanding, and Music Cognition," in *The Oxford Handbook of Critical Improvisation Studies*, ed. George E. Lewis and Benjamin Piekut (New York: Oxford University Press, 2016), 74–90.

38. Hagberg, "Jazz Improvisation," 260–61. Regarding recognizing the subject as distinct from oneself, Hagberg writes, "we have to see that life as *that* life, as one possessing an autonomy from our own interests, drives, ambitions and concerns. That person as viewed by us may of course become relationally intertwined with all or any of these . . . but the essence of humane acknowledgement is found in our foundational recognition of their autonomy or moral independence from us" (262).
39. One of the virtues of musical education that many educators highlight is the honing of these skills of attunement to the other.
40. Hagberg, "Jazz Improvisation," 282.
41. When discussing virtues such as empathy, it is crucial to recognize how these notions can be defined in ableist ways. Melanie Yergeau discusses how the dominant view of autistic people as lacking a theory of mind defines them as incapable of empathy. She writes: "Disempathy is our collective story, and through this story of disempathy, autistic collectivity ceases to exist." Melanie Yergeau, "Occupying Autism: Rhetoric, Involuntarity, and the Meaning of Autistic Lives," in *Occupying Disability: Critical Approaches to Community, Justice, and Decolonizing Disability*, ed. Pamela Block et al. (New York: Springer, 2016), 87. When considering virtues, it is important to consider not only *how* they are cultivated but also how ableist assumptions can make these very virtues inaccessible to certain groups.
42. Alasdair MacIntyre, *Dependent Rational Animals* (Chicago: Open Court, 1999). For a discussion of the way MacIntyre addresses disability in this text, see Licia Carlson, "Rethinking Normalcy, Normalization and Cognitive Disability," in *Science and Other Cultures: Issues in the Philosophy of Science and Technology*, ed. Sandra Harding and Robert Figueroa (New York: Routledge, 2003), 154–71.
43. Kittay, *Learning from My Daughter*; Eva Kittay, "Ideal Theory, Bioethics, and the Exclusion of People with Severe Disabilities," in *Naturalized Bioethics: Toward Responsible Knowing and Practice*, ed. Hilde Lindemann, Marian Verkerk, and Margaret Urban Walker (Cambridge: Cambridge University Press, 2012), 218–37; Eva Kittay, "On the Margins of Moral Personhood," *Ethics* 116 (2005): 100–131. See also Carlson, *Faces*.
44. I address numerous forms of ignorance that attend philosophical discussions of intellectual disability in Carlson, *Faces*, 201–4.
45. Hagberg, "Jazz Improvisation," 265.
46. Marcel, *Being and Having*, 117.
47. Higgins, *Music between Us*, also talks about musical solidarity across cultures.
48. Levinson, *Musical Concerns*, 81.
49. Warren, *Music*, 162.

50. Warren, *Music and Ethical Responsibility*, 187. Wayne Bowman points out that the ethical significance of musical encounters is not guaranteed: "each and every one of these claims is contingent. They accrue to musical endeavors and experiences of certain kinds, under certain circumstances. None follows automatically from the facts of our having taught music or having been engaged in it." Wayne Bowman, "The Ethical Significance of Music-Making," *Music Education Now*, https://jfin107.wordpress.com/scholarly-paper-the-ethical-significance-of-music-making-by-wayne-bowman/.
51. Perring, "Facilitation," 186.
52. See note 37 in chapter 2.
53. In *Musicophilia*, Oliver Sacks speaks about conditions like *amusia* that make musical experience painful for people (Ch. 10). H. M. Evans talks about his experience of musical intrusions as a source of profound suffering in "Music in Body and Imagination," in *The Oxford Handbook of Music and the Body*, ed. Youn Kim and Sander Gilman (Oxford University Press, 2019), 349–64.
54. Alper, *Giving Voice*.
55. Watts and Ridley, "Identities," 364.

Conclusion

1. Philip Alperson, "Facing the Music: Voices from the Margins," *Topoi* 28 (1991): 91–96; Goehr, *Imaginary Museum*; Alperson and Carroll, "Music, Mind, and Morality"; Susan McClary, *Feminine Endings: Music, Gender, and Sexuality* (Minneapolis: University of Minnesota Press, 1991).
2. Rosemarie Garland Thomson, *Extraordinary Bodies* (New York: Columbia University Press, 2017). Thomson defines the *normate* as "the constructed identity of those who, by way of bodily configurations and cultural capital they assume, can step into a position of authority and wield the power it grants them" (8). For example, Jennifer Robinson makes reference to the "qualified listener" and "normal folk" when speaking about perceiving art. Robinson, *Deeper Than Reason*, 348–49, 290–91. She is certainly not unique in doing so, but how might challenging this change the questions that philosophers of music ask and answer?
3. Honisch, "Virtuosities," 279. For a fuller discussion of Tsujii, see Stefan Sunandan Honisch, "Different Eyes, Ears, Bodies: Pianist Nobuyuki Tsujii and the Education of the Sensorium through Musical Performance," PhD diss., University of British Columbia, 2016.
4. I am not arguing here that musicking somehow justifies the claim that "we are *all* disabled." For various interdisciplinary perspectives on what it means to claim we are all disabled, see Licia Carlson and Matthew Murray, eds., *The Boundaries of Disability: Critical Reflections* (New York: Routledge, 2021).
5. Helen Meekosha, "Decolonising Disability: Thinking and Acting Globally," *Disability & Society* 26, no. 6 (2011): 667–82.

6. Sami Schalk and Jina B. Kim, "Integrating Race, Transforming Feminist Disability Studies," *Signs* 46, no. 1 (2020): 31–55.
7. Straus, *Extraordinary Measures*; Straus, "Idiots Savants."
8. I have found Gary Ansdell's work enormously helpful, as he addresses many of the same themes and ideas from the perspective of music therapy in ways that complement many of my own philosophical ideas. Ansdell, *How Music Helps*.
9. One example of this is with regard to research ethics. When considering research on the musical lives of people with intellectual disabilities, there are complex methodological and ethical questions that require serious consideration. See Licia Carlson, "Research Ethics and Intellectual Disability: Broadening the Debates," *Yale Journal of Biology and Medicine* 86, no. 3 (2013): 303–13; Reetta Mietola, Sonja Miettinen, and Simo Vehmas, "Voiceless Subjects? Research Ethics and Persons with Profound Intellectual Disabilities," *International Journal of Social Research Methodology* 20, no. 3 (2017): 263–74, https://doi.org/10.1080/13645579.2017.1287872.
10. Minette Mans defines musical worlds as "culturally informed systems of musical thinking and creating." She locates the boundaries of musical worlds culturally, writing that "a musical world may be seen as something common to musical cultures everywhere but with the differences of musical content and the societal values that are drawn upon the landscape. A musical world encompasses all our sonic knowledge, choices, aesthetic preferences, and memories. It refers broadly to customs of musical practice based on a system of knowledge, understanding, and behaviors brought about by individual and collective musical experiences within a given cultural context(s)." Minette Manns, *Living in Worlds of Music: A View of Education and Values* (Dordrecht: Springer, 2009), 14.
11. Eva Kittay, "The Moral Significance of Being Human," *Proceedings and Addresses of the APA* 91 (2017): 38.
12. Vorhaus, *Giving Voice*. He gives two reasons for this. He states: "we are justified in treating some people as if they have the potential to participate when that potential is in doubt." First, "the effects of being treated as an outsider, as sub-human or as a non-citizen are often disastrous and lifelong" (43). Secondly, "If we treat people with profound disabilities as if they have the potential to participate, we, and they, are liable to make more effort than otherwise to develop their capacities; equally, if we treat people as if they lack all such potential, we lose an incentive to make every effort to encourage them to realise whatever potential they have" (43). Of participation, he says, "I construe 'sharing' as 'participating in,' and 'common life' as the social life characteristic of the environment someone lives in" (33).

Coda

1. https://www.janswinburne.com/blog/.
2. https://www.janswinburne.com/blog/.

References

Alper, Meryl. *Giving Voice: Mobile Communication, Disability, and Inequality.* Cambridge, MA: MIT Press, 2017.

Alperson, Philip. "Facing the Music: Voices from the Margins." *Topoi* 28 (1991): 91–96.

Alperson, Philip, and Noel Carroll. "Music, Mind, and Morality: Arousing the Body Politic." *Journal of Aesthetic Education* 42, no. 1 (Spring 2008): 1–15.

Ansdell, Gary. *How Music Helps in Music Therapy and Everyday Life.* New York: Routledge, 2015.

Bakan, Michael. "Toward an Ethnographic Model of Disability in the Ethnomusicology of Autism." In *The Oxford Handbook of Music and Disability Studies*, edited by Blake Howe, Stephanie Jensen-Moulton, Neil Lerner, and Joseph Straus, 15–36. New York: Oxford University Press, 2015.

Bakan, Michael, with Mara Chasar, Graeme Gibson, Elizabeth J. Grace, Zena Hamelson, Dotan Nitzberg, Gordon Peterson, Maureen Pytlik, Donald Rindale, Amy Sequenzia, and Addison Star. *Music and Autism: Speaking for Ourselves.* New York: Oxford University Press, 2018.

Barenboim, Daniel, and Edward W. Said. *Parallels and Paradoxes: Explorations in Music and Society.* New York: Pantheon, 2002.

Benson, Bruce. *The Improvisation of Musical Dialogue: A Phenomenology of Music.* Cambridge: Cambridge University Press, 2003.

Berne, Patricia, Aurora Levins Morales, David Langstaff, and Sins Invalid. "Ten Principles of Disability Justice." *WSQ: Women's Studies Quarterly* 46, nos. 1–2 (Spring/Summer 2018): 227–30.

Block, Pamela, Devva Kasnitz, Akemi Nishida, and Nick Pollard. *Occupying Disability: Critical Approaches to Community, Justice, and Decolonizing Disability.* New York: Springer 2016.

Bowman, Wayne. "The ethical significance of music-making." *Music Education Now.* https://jfin107.wordpress.com/scholarly-paper-the-ethical-significance-of-music-making-by-wayne-bowman/

Brann, Eva. *The Music of the Republic.* Philadelphia: Paul Dry, 2004.

Barrass, Stephen, Michael Whitelaw, and Guillaume Potard, "Listening to the Mind Listening: Practice Based Research in EEG Sonification." *Media International Australia Incorporating Culture and Policy* 118, no. 1 (2006): 60. http://doi.org/10.1177/1329878 X0611800109

Cameron, Lindsay. *The Music of Light: The Extraordinary Story of Kenzaburo and Hikari Oe.* New York: Free Press, 1998.

Carlson, Licia. "Encounters with Musical Others." In *Phenomenology and the Arts*, edited by Licia Carlson and Peter Costello, 234–52. Lanham, MD: Lexington, 2015.

Carlson, Licia. *The Faces of Intellectual Disability.* Bloomington: Indiana University Press, 2009.

Carlson, Licia. "Musical Becoming: Intellectual Disability and the Transformative Power of Music." In *Foundations of Disability Studies*, edited by Matthew Wappett and Katrina Arndt, 83–103. London: Palgrave Macmillan, 2013.

Carlson, Licia. "Music, Intellectual Disability, and Human Flourishing." In *The Oxford Handbook of Music and Disability Studies*, edited by Blake Howe, Stephanie Jensen-Moulton, Neil Lerner, and Joseph Straus, 37–53. New York: Oxford University Press, 2015.

Carlson, Licia. "On Moral Status and Intellectual Disability: Challenging and Expanding the Debates." In *The Oxford Handbook of Philosophy and Disability*, edited by Adam Cureton and David Wasserman, 482–97. New York: Oxford University Press, 2019.

Carlson, Licia. "Research Ethics and Intellectual Disability: Broadening the Debates." *Yale Journal of Biology and Medicine* 86, no. 3 (2013): 303–13.

Carlson, Licia. "Rethinking Normalcy, Normalization and Cognitive Disability." In *Science and Other Cultures: Issues in the Philosophy of Science and Technology*, edited by Sandra Harding and Robert Figueroa, 154–71. New York: Routledge, 2003.

Carlson, Licia. "Who's the Expert? Rethinking Authority in Light of Intellectual Disability." *Journal of Intellectual Disability Research* 54, supp. 1 (March 2010): 58–65.

Carlson, Licia. "Feminism and Disability Theory." In *The Oxford Handbook of Feminist Philosophy*, edited by Kim Hall and Ásta Sveinsdóttir), 516–30. New York: Oxford University Press, 2021.

Carlson, Licia, and Matthew Murray, eds. *The Boundaries of Disability: Critical Reflections*. New York: Routledge, 2021.

Carlson, Licia, and Sandra Sufian. "Thoughts on Precarity, Risk, and Disablement during COVID-19." In *The Boundaries of Disability: Critical Reflections*, edited by Licia Carlson and Matthew Murray, 124–137. New York: Routledge, 2020.

Cassuto, Leonard. "Oliver Sacks: The P. T. Barnum of the Postmodern World?" *American Quarterly* 53, no. 2 (June 2000): 326–33.

Cassuto, Leonard. "The Uncanny Symphony of Oliver Sacks." *Chronicle of Higher Education*, November 2, 2007. https://www.chronicle.com/article/the-uncanny-symphony-of-oliver-sacks/?cid2=gen_login_refresh&cid=gen_sign_in.

Cheng, William. *Just Vibrations: The Purpose of Sounding Good*. Ann Arbor: University of Michigan, 2016.

Cheung, Stephanie, Elizabeth Han, Azadeh Kushki, Evdokia Anagnostou, and Elaine Biddiss. "Biomusic: An Auditory Interface for Detecting Physiological Indicators of Anxiety in Children." *Frontiers in Neuroscience* 10 (2016): 401. https://doi.org/10.3389/fnins.2016.00401.

Cummings, Naomi. *The Sonic Self*. Bloomington: Indiana University Press, 2000.

Davis, Angela. *Blues Legacies and Black Feminism*. New York: Vintage, 1999.

DeNora, Tia. *Music Asylums: Wellbeing through Music in Everyday Life*. Farnham, UK: Ashgate, 2013.

Douglass, Frederick. *Narrative of the Life of Frederick Douglass*. London: Penguin Classics, 2016.

Dufrenne, Mikel. *The Phenomenology of Aesthetic Experience*. Evanston, IL: Northeastern University Press, 1973.

Evans, H. M. "Music in Body and Imagination." In *The Oxford Handbook of Music and the Body*, edited by Youn Kim and Sander Gilman, 349–64. New York: Oxford University Press, 2019.

Foucault, Michel. "What Is an Author?" In *Michel Foucault: Aesthetics, Method and Epistemology*, edited by James D. Faubion, 204–22. New York: New Press, 1998.

Friedman, Margie, and Barbara Multer-Wellin, dirs. *Orchestrating Change*. PBS, 2021. https://orchestratingchangethefilm.com.

Gardner, Howard. *Intelligence Reframed: Multiple Intelligences for the 21st Century*. New York: Basic Books, 2000.

Gass, William. *Reading Rilke: Reflections on the Problems of Translation*. New York: Basic Books, 1999.

Gibney, Elizabeth. "How One Astronomer Hears the Universe." *Nature* 577 (January 2020): 155.

Glennie, Evelyn, Sander L. Gilman, and Youn Kim. "Is There Disabled Music? Music and the Body from Dame Evelyn Glennie's Perspective." In *The Oxford Handbook of Music and the Body*, edited by Youn Kim and Sander L. Gilman, 318–30. New York: Oxford University Press, 2019.

Goehr, Lydia. *The Imaginary Museum of Musical Works: An Essay in the Philosophy of Music*. Oxford: Oxford University Press, 2007.

Grant, M. J. "The Illogical Logic of Music Torture." *Torture* 23, no. 2 (2013): 4–13.

Hagberg, Garry. "Jazz Improvisation and Ethical Interaction: A Sketch of the Connections." In *Art and Ethical Criticism*, edited by Gary Hagberg, 259–85. Malden, MA: Blackwell, 2008.

Hall, Kim ed., *Feminist Disability Studies*. Bloomington: Indiana University Press, 2011.

Hambrook, Colin. "Molly Joyce on the Influence of Disability Studies on Her Music-Making." *Disability Arts Online*, June 1, 2019. https://disabilityarts.online/magazine/opinion/molly-joyce/.

Hanslick, Eduard. *On the Musically Beautiful*. Translated by Geoffrey Payzant. Indianapolis, IL: Hackett Publishing, 1996.

Harper, Ralph. *On Presence: Variations and Reflections*. Philadelphia: Trinity Press International, 1991.

Higgins, Kathleen. *The Music of Our Lives*. Lanham, MD: Lexington, 2011.

Higgins, Kathleen. *The Music between Us: Is Music a Universal Language?* Chicago: University of Chicago Press, 2014.

Honisch, Stefan Sunandan. "Different Eyes, Ears, Bodies: Pianist Nobuyuki Tsujii and the Education of the Sensorium through Musical Performance." PhD diss., University of British Columbia, 2016.

Honisch, Stefan Sunandan. "'Re-narrating Disability' through Musical Performance." *Music Theory Online* 15, nos. 3–4 (August 2009). https://mtosmt.org/issues/mto.09.15.3/mto.09.15.3.honisch.html.

Honisch, Stefan Sunandan. "Virtuosities of Deafness and Blindness: Musical Performance and the Prized Body." In *The Oxford Handbook of Music and the Body*, edited by Youn Kim and Sander L. Gilman, 276–94. New York: Oxford University Press, 2019.

Howe, Blake. "Disabling Music Performance." In *The Oxford Handbook of Music and Disability Studies*, edited by Blake Howe, Stephanie Jensen-Moulton, Neil Lerner, and Joseph Straus, 191–209. New York: Oxford University Press, 2015.

Howe, Blake, Stephanie Jensen-Moulton, Neil Lerner, and Joseph Straus, eds. *The Oxford Handbook of Music and Disability Studies*. New York: Oxford University Press, 2015.

Husserl, Edmund. *The Phenomenology of Internal Time-Consciousness*. Edited by Martin Heidegger, translated by James Churchill. Bloomington: Indiana University Press, 1964.

Ingarden, Roman. *Ontology of the Work of Art*. Athens: University of Ohio Press, 1998.

Iyer, Vijay. "Exploding the Narrative in Jazz Improvisation." In *Uptown Conversations: The New Jazz Studies*, edited by Robert O'Meally, Brent Hayes Edwards, and Farah Jasmine Griffin, 393–403. New York: Columbia University Press, 2004.

Iyer, Vijay. "Improvisation, Action Understanding, and Music Cognition." In *The Oxford Handbook of Critical Improvisation Studies*, edited by George E. Lewis and Benjamin Piekut, 74–90. New York: Oxford University Press, 2016.

Iyer, Vijay. "The Myth of the Solitary Listener: Music Cognition and the Humanities." Unpublished keynote address delivered at the annual meeting of New England Music Cognition Group. Harvard University, 2016.

Iyer, Vijay. "On Improvisation, Temporality, and Embodied Experience." In *Sound Unbound: Sampling Digital Music and Culture*, edited by Paul D. Miller, 273–92. Cambridge: MIT Press, 2008.

Kafer, Alison. *Feminist, Queer, Crip*. Bloomington: Indiana University Press, 2013.

Kim, Youn, and Sander L. Gilman, eds. *The Oxford Handbook of Music and the Body*. New York: Oxford University Press, 2019.

Kittay, Eva. "Ideal Theory, Bioethics, and the Exclusion of People with Severe Disabilities." In *Naturalized Bioethics: Toward Responsible Knowing and Practice*, edited by Hilde Lindemann, Marian Verkerk, and Margaret Urban Walker, 218–37. Cambridge: Cambridge University Press, 2012.

Kittay, Eva. *Learning from My Daughter: The Value and Care of Disabled Minds*. Oxford: Oxford University Press, 2019.

Kittay, Eva. "The Moral Significance of Being Human. *Proceedings and Addresses of the APA* 91 (2017): 22–42.

Kittay, Eva. "On the Margins of Moral Personhood." *Ethics* 116 (2005): 100–131.

Kittay, Eva, and Licia Carlson, eds. *Cognitive Disability and Its Challenge to Moral Philosophy*. Malden, MA: Wiley-Blackwell, 2010.

Kittay, Jeffrey. "The Sound Surround: Exploring How One Might Design the Everyday Soundscape for the Truly Captive Audience." *Nordic Journal of Music Therapy* 17, no. 1 (2008): 41–54.

Kivy, Peter. "Musical Morality." *Revue Internationale de Philosophie* 4 (2009): 397–412.

Kleege, Georgina. *More Than Meets the Eye: What Blindness Brings to Art*. New York: Oxford University Press, 2018.

Lange, Lynda, ed. *Feminist Interpretations of Jean-Jacques Rousseau*. University Park: Pennsylvania State University Press, 2002.

Lenhoff, Howard M., Olegario Perales, and Gregory Hickok. "Absolute Pitch in Williams Syndrome." *Music Perception* 18, no. 4 (2001): 491–503.

Lerner, Neil, and Joseph Straus, eds. *Sounding Off: Theorizing Disability in Music*. New York: Routledge, 2006.

Levi, Primo. *Survival in Auschwitz*. Translated by Stuart Woolf. New York: Simon & Schuster, 1995.

Levinson, Jerrold. *Musical Concerns: Essays in Philosophy of Music*. Oxford: Oxford University Press, 2015.

Levinson, Jerrold, and Philip Alperson. "What Is a Temporal Art"? In Jerrold Levinson, *Musical Concerns: Essays in Philosophy of Music*, 155–70. Oxford: Oxford University Press, 2015.

Levitin, Daniel, and Ursula Belugi. "Musical Abilities in Individuals with Williams Syndrome." *Music Perception* 15, no. 4 (1998): 357–89.

Linton, Simi. "Disability Studies, Not Disability Studies." *Disability and Society* 13, no. 4 (1998): 525–40.

Lubet, Alex. *Music, Disability, and Society*. Philadelphia: Temple University Press, 2011.

Lugones, Maria. "Playfulness, 'World'-Travelling, and Loving Perception." In *Feminist Social Thought: A Reader*, edited by Diana Tietjens Meyer, 147–59. New York: Routledge, 1989.

Macdonald, Raymond, David J. Hargreaves, and Dorothy Miell, eds. *The Oxford Handbook of Musical Identities*. New York: Oxford University Press, 2017.

MacGregor, John M. *Metamorphisis: The Fiber Art of Judith Scott*. Oakland, CA: Creative Growth Art Center, 1999.

MacIntyre, Alasdair. *Dependent Rational Animals*. Chicago: Open Court, 1999.

Mairs, Nancy. *Waist-High in the World: A Life among the Nondisabled*. Boston: Beacon, 1996.

Majithia, Roopen. "Blues and Catharsis." In *Blues Philosophy for Everyone: Thinking Deep about Feeling Low*, edited by Jesse R. Steinberg and Abrol Fairweather, 84–93. Malden, MA: Wiley-Blackwell, 2012.

Manns, Minette. *Living in Worlds of Music: A View of Education and Values*. Dordrecht: Springer, 2009.

Marcel, Gabriel. *Being and Having*. Translated by Katharine Farrer. Westminster, UK: Dacre, 1949.

Marcel, Gabriel. *Music and Philosophy*. Translated by Stephen Maddux and Robert E. Wood. Milwaukee: Marquette University Press, 2005.

McClary, Susan. *Feminine Endings: Music, Gender, and Sexuality*. Minneapolis: University of Minnesota Press, 1991.

McKay, George. *Shakin' All Over: Popular Music and Disability*. Ann Arbor: University of Michigan Press, 2013.

Meekosha, Helen. "Decolonising Disability: Thinking and Acting Globally." *Disability & Society* 26, no. 6 (2011): 667–82.

Mietola, Reetta, Sonja Miettinen, and Simo Vehmas. "Voiceless Subjects? Research Ethics and Persons with Profound Intellectual Disabilities." *International Journal of Social Research Methodology* 20, no. 3 (2017): 263–74. https://doi.org/10.1080/13645579.2017.1287872.

Moore, Leroy F. Jr., Tiny aka Lisa Gray-Garcia, and Emmitt H. Thrower. "Black & Blue: Policing Disability & Poverty beyond Occupy." In *Occupying Disability: Critical Approaches to Community, Justice, and Decolonizing Disability*, edited by Pamela Block, Devva Kasnitz, Akemi Nishida, and Nick Pollard, 295–318. New York: Springer, 2016.

Neruda, Pablo. *All the Odes*. Edited by Ilan Stavans. New York: Farrar, Straus and Giroux, 2013.

Nietzsche, Friedrich. *The Dionysian Vision of the World*. Translated by Ira J. Allen. Minneapolis: Univocal, 2013.

Nietzsche, Friedrich. *The Will to Power*. Translated by Walter Kaufmann. New York: Vintage, 1967.

O'Dea, Jane. "Virtue in Musical Performance." *Journal of Aesthetic Education* 27, no. 1 (Spring 1993): 51–62.

Pavlicevic, Mercedes, Gary Ansdell, and Evan Ruud, eds. *Community Music Therapy*. London: Jessica Kingsley, 2014.

Perring, Giles. "The Facilitation of Learning-Disabled Arts: A Cultural Perspective." In *Bodies in Commotion*, edited by Carrie Sandahl and Philip Auslander, 175–89. Ann Arbor: University of Michigan Press, 2005.

Preisler, Jerome, with the Trush family. *Daniel's Music: One Family's Journey from Tragedy to Empowerment through Faith, Medicine, and the Healing Power of Music.* New York: Skyhorse, 2015.

Price, Margaret. "The Bodymind Problem and the Possibilities of Pain." *Hypatia* 30, no. 1 (2014): 268–84.

Radano, Ronald M., and Phillip V. Bohlman, eds. *Music and the Racial Imagination.* Chicago: University of Chicago Press, 2001.

Rink, John. "Impersonating the Music in Performance." In *The Oxford Handbook of Musical Identities*, edited by Raymond Macdonald, David J. Hargreaves, and Dorothy Miell, 345–63. New York: Oxford University Press, 2017.

Robinson, Jennifer. *Deeper Than Reason: Emotion and Its Role in Literature, Music, and Art.* New York: Oxford University Press, 2005.

Rousseau, Jean-Jacques. *Essay on the Origin of Languages and Writings Related to Music.* Translated by John T. Scott. Hanover, NH: Dartmouth College Press, 1998.

Sacks, Oliver. *Musicophilia: Tales of Music and the Brain.* New York: Vintage, 2008.

Sandahl, Carrie, and Philip Auslander, eds. *Bodies in Commotion.* Ann Arbor: University of Michigan Press, 2005.

Schalk, Sami. "Coming to Claim Crip: Disidentification with/in Disability Studies." *Disability Studies Quarterly* 33, no. 2 (2013). https://doi.org/10.18061/dsq.v33i2.3705.

Schalk, Sami, and Jina B. Kim. "Integrating Race, Transforming Feminist Disability Studies." *Signs: Journal of Women in Culture and Society* 46, no. 1 (2020): 31–55.

Schutz, Alfred. "Making Music Together: A Study in Social Relationship." *Social Research* 18, no. 1 (1951): 76–97.

Sforza, Terry, with Howard and Sylvia Lenhoff. *The Strangest Song: One Father's Quest to Help His Daughter Find Her Voice.* Amherst, NY: Prometheus, 2006.

Siebers, Tobin. *Disability Aesthetics.* Ann Arbor: University of Michigan Press, 2010.

Small, Christopher. *Musicking: The Meanings of Performing and Listening.* Middletown, CT: Wesleyan University Press, 1998.

Sörbom, Göran. "Aristotle on Music as Representation." In *Musical Worlds: New Directions in the Philosophy of Music*, edited by Philip Alperson, 37–46. University Park: Pennsylvania State University Press, 1998.

Steinberg, Jesse R., and Abrol Fairweather, eds. *Blues Philosophy for Everyone: Thinking Deep about Feeling Low.* Malden, MA: Wiley-Blackwell, 2012.

Straus, Joseph. *Broken Beauty: Musical Modernism and the Representation of Disability.* Oxford: Oxford University Press, 2018.

Straus, Joseph. *Extraordinary Measures: Disability in Music.* New York: Oxford University Press, 2011.

Straus, Joseph. "Idiots Savants, Retarded Savants, Talented Aments, Mono-Savants, Autistic Savants, Just Plain Savants, People with Savant Syndrome, and Autistic People Who Are Good at Things: A View from Disability Studies." *Disability Studies Quarterly* 34, no. 3 (2014). https://doi.org/10.18061/dsq.v34i3.3407

Supper, Alexandra. "Sublime Frequencies: The Construction of Sublime Listening Experiences in the Sonification of Scientific Data." *Social Studies of Science* 44, no. 1 (2014): 34–58.

Taruskin, Richard. *Text and Act: Essays on Musical Performance*. Oxford: Oxford University Press, 1995.
Thomson, Rosemarie Garland. "Feminist Disability Studies." *Signs: Journal of Women in Culture and Society* 30, no. 2 (2005): 1557–87.
Thomson, Rosemarie Garland. "The Case for Conserving Disability." *Journal of Bioethical Inquiry* 9 (September 2012): 339–55.
Thomson, Rosemarie Garland. *Extraordinary Bodies*. New York: Columbia University Press, 2017.
Thomson, Rosemarie Garland. "Misfits: A Feminist Materialist Disability Concept." *Hypatia* 26, no. 3 (Summer 2011): 591–609. https://doi.org/10.1111/j.1527-2001.2011.01206.x.
Tremain, Shelley ed. "Special Issue: Improving Feminist Philosophy and Theory by Taking Account of Disability," *Disability Studies Quarterly* 33, no. 4 (2013). https://doi.org/10.18061/dsq.v33i4
Trent, James. *Inventing the Feeble Mind: A History of Intellectual Disability in the United States*. Oxford: Oxford University Press, 2016.
Tsiris, George. "Voices from the 'Ghetto': Music Therapy Perspectives on Disability and Music (A Response to Joseph Straus's Book *Extraordinary Measures: Disability in Music*)." *International Journal of Community Music* 6 (2013): 334–42.
Unwin, Stephen. "The Sound of Silence: My Joey Does Not Need to Speak to Be Heard." *Byline Times*, September 17, 2021. https://bylinetimes.com/2021/09/17/the-sound-of-silence-my-joey-doesnt-need-to-speak-to-be-heard/
Vorhaus, John. *Giving Voice to Profound Disability: Dignity, Dependence and Human Capabilities*. London: Routledge, 2016.
Vorhaus, John, and Adam Ockelford. "Identity and Musical Development in People with Severe Profound and Multiple Learning Disabilities." In *The Oxford Handbook of Musical Identities*, edited by Raymond Macdonald, David J. Hargreaves, and Dorothy Miell, 642–67. New York: Oxford University Press, 2017.
Warren, Jeff. *Music and Ethical Responsibility*. Cambridge: Cambridge University Press, 2014.
Watts, Michael, and Barbara Ridley. "Identities of Dis/ability and Music." *British Educational Research Journal* 38, no. 3 (2012): 353–72.
Wendell, Susan. *The Rejected Body: Feminist Philosophical Reflections on Disability*. New York: Routledge, 1996.
West, Cornel. "Black Strivings in a Twilight Civilization." In Cornel West, *The Cornel West Reader*, 87–118. New York: Basic Civitas, 1999.
Wittgenstein, Ludwig. *Culture and Value*. Edited by G. H. Von Wright, translated by Peter Winch. Chicago: University of Chicago Press, 1980.
Yergeau, Melanie. "Occupying Autism: Rhetoric, Involuntarity, and the Meaning of Autistic Lives." In *Occupying Disability: Critical Approaches to Community, Justice, and Decolonizing Disability*, edited by Pamela Block, Devva Kasnitz, Akemi Nishida, and Nick Pollard, 83–95. New York: Springer, 2016.
Zwicky, Jan. *Lyric Philosophy*. Edmonton: Brush Education, 2014.
Zwicky, Jan. "What Is Lyric Philosophy? An Introduction." *Common Knowledge* 20, no. 1 (Winter 2014): 14–27.

Index

For the benefit of digital users, indexed terms that span two pages (e.g., 52–53) may, on occasion, appear on only one of those pages.

ableism, x, 52–53, 73–74, 76, 78–79, 93n.25, 104n.41
abnormal, 32–33, 46–47, 50, 68
aesthetics
   disability, 3–4, 49, 78
   Western, 3
autism (ASD), autistic persons, 7, 15, 16–17, 32, 41–42, 49–50, 95n.56, 99n.47, 103n.26

Benson, Bruce, 15, 16, 23
blues, 28, 32–33, 61–62, 92–93n.23, 93–94n.35

communication, 10–11, 25–26, 32–33, 40–42, 55, 58, 61, 67, 71–72, 75–76. *See also* self-expression
composers, 4, 10–11, 13, 15–16, 21, 25–26, 32–18, 41, 43, 45, 46, 53, 67, 68–69, 72–73, 78, 91n.8
critical disability studies, 6–7, 77–78
culture, 8, 28, 29–30, 44–45, 47–49, 57, 78, 79–80, 106n.10
   barriers, 39
   disability, 6–7, 49
Cummings, Naomi, 20–21

deafness, 30–31, 49–50, 56–57, 100n.3
decolonization, 78
dehumanization, 2–3, 8–9, 11, 37, 40, 41–42, 52–53, 96n.2
dementia, 7, 27–28
DeNora, Tia, 10–11, 26–27, 28, 35, 64
dependence, 12, 56, 66–67, 72–73
difference, 6–7, 11, 29–30, 44–51, 53, 58, 60, 69, 77, 80

disability, 3–5, 8–10, 29–35, 49, 50–53, 55, 56, 75–76, 78–79
   arts, 3–4, 29–35, 48–49, 51, 75, 76, 78
   culture, 49
   definitions of, 6–7, 73–74, 94n.49
   as generative, 29–30, 32, 48, 55
   intellectual and cognitive disability, 2–4, 7, 8–9, 11–12, 27–28, 31, 32–34, 35, 37, 40–44, 46–48, 49–51, 52–53, 54, 63, 67, 79–80
   learning, 32, 94n.49
   medical model of, 6–7, 78–79
   models of, 6–7, 43–44, 51–52, 79
   overcoming, 29–30, 32–33, 43–44, 64
   as performative, 8, 10–11, 29–35
   personal tragedy model of, 6–7, 43–44, 49, 68
   physical, 29–31
   profound, 11, 33–34, 37, 41, 42–43, 56, 65, 67, 76, 106n.12
   rights, 6–7
   terminology, 7
disability studies, 3–4, 12, 51–52, 72, 77–78, 79, 94n.38
   Feminist, 8, 72, 78, 89n.20

embodiment, 3, 6–7, 8, 10–11, 19–21, 24–25, 26, 27, 30–31, 35, 49, 55, 71, 77–78, 81–82
emotion, 24, 26, 27–28, 32, 33–34, 41–42, 43, 61, 77–78, 92–93n.23
empathy, 12, 41–42, 71–72, 80
epistemic
   authority, 51, 73
   barriers, 11, 66

epistemic (*cont.*)
  force of musical experience, 36–53
  injustice, 78–79
  value, 5, 9

feminism, 8, 28, 72, 78, 88n.8
finitude, 23, 24
flourishing, 3–4, 28, 33–34, 35, 49, 51, 55, 64–67, 74, 75, 80
Foucault, Michel, 17–18, 34–35

Garland Thomson, Rosemarie, 8, 77–78
gesture, 20, 21, 25–26, 57–58, 61, 63, 71–72
Glennie, Evelyne, 30–31, 56–57

Hagberg, Garry, 24, 71, 72, 73–74
Harper, Ralph, 69–70
hearing, 30–31, 50–51
  autistic, 49–50
  disablist, 49–50
  normal, 49–50
Higgins, Kathleen, 3, 19, 23–24, 33–34, 38–40, 49, 62, 64, 71
Hip Hop, 48–49
Honisch, Stefan, 29–30, 77–78
Howe, Blake, 29–31, 45–46
humility, 12, 52–53, 73–74
Husserl, Edmund, 22

identity, 6–7, 10, 19, 25–26, 27–28, 30–31, 39–40, 44–45, 68, 91n.3
  sonic, 30–31, 94–95n.50
improvisation, 24, 25–26, 27, 71, 72, 73–74
Ingarden, Roman, 15
instruments, 10, 13–14, 20, 30–31, 69–70, 72–73, 76, 99–100n.50
intellectually disabled persons, x, 8–9, 11, 31, 33–34, 35, 40–44, 52–53, 55, 56, 63, 65, 66–69, 70–71, 72–74, 75, 77, 79, 80. *See* intellectual and cognitive disability
interdependence, 66–67, 72–73, 74
Iyer, Vijay, 21, 26, 38, 50, 71

Jazz, 21, 24, 25–26, 30–31, 38, 71, 72, 73–74

joy, musical, 12, 19, 24, 33–34, 35, 42, 64–67, 68, 71, 74, 75
Joyce, Molly, 30–31
justice, 9, 81–82
  disability justice, ix, 5, 76

Kittay, Eva, 55, 65, 66–67, 73–74, 79–80
Kivy, Peter, 11, 36–37, 41, 70
knowledge. *See* epistemic
  about disability, 51–52, 78
  about other human subjects, 5, 11, 36–53
  moral, 11, 36–53
  musical, 65–66, 106n.10
  self-knowledge, 5, 10–11, 20–25

language, 7, 11, 32, 37–38, 41–42, 55–58, 59, 66, 77–78, 81–82, 95n.58
Levinas, Emanuel, 69–70
Levinson, Jerrold, 19, 21–22, 39–40, 41, 74
loss, 54–55

Marcel, Gabriel, 27, 58–59, 73–74
memory, 27–28, 46–47, 54–55
mental illness, 31
Moore, Leroy, 48–49
music
  absolute, 11, 25, 36, 70, 96–97n.4
  African-American, Black, 28, 48, 61–62
  cross-cultural, 39, 49, 53, 78, 79–80
  epistemic force of, 11, 36–53
  humanizing, 11, 37–46, 52–53, 60
  as performative, 8, 29–35, 77–78
  as restorative, 10–11, 26–29
  weaponized, torture, 9, 28–29, 75, 96n.2
music therapy, 3–4, 9–10, 26–27, 28, 35, 43, 51–52, 66, 76, 78–79
musical asylum, 10–11, 26–27, 28–29, 35, 57, 64, 102n.13
musical we, 12, 13, 56, 58, 60–76, 77, 80
musical work, 3, 8, 10, 11, 13, 15–18, 19, 20, 21, 24, 36–37, 46, 49, 54–55, 57, 62, 65, 70, 79–80

musicking, 6, 8–9, 12, 21–22, 24–31, 32, 35, 37, 40, 41, 44–45, 46, 47, 49–50, 51, 52, 53, 58, 60–61, 66–67, 68–70, 74, 75, 76, 77–78, 79–80
mystery, 9, 58–59, 69–70, 73–74, 81–82

narrative, 33–34, 44–45, 73–74, 80
  musical, 16–17, 21, 25, 73–74
Neruda, Pablo, 13–14
neurodiversity, 7, 49–50
Nietzsche, Friedrich, 55, 57–58, 66
non-disabled (temporarily-abled), 8, 30–31, 44, 51, 55, 75, 88n.6
normal, 30–31, 34, 44–45, 49–50, 58, 62–63, 68, 77–78, 99n.48
normalization, 9–10, 34, 51, 58, 64

Oe, Hikari, 32–33, 40, 43
oppression, 6–7, 10–11, 26–27, 28, 40, 52, 93n.33
other, othering, 8–9, 10, 34–35, 36, 37, 39–40, 44, 46–47, 53, 58, 60, 61, 75, 80, 95n.54
  musical others, 10, 13–18, 61

pandemic, ix, 63
performers, 10–11, 13, 15–16, 17–18, 21–23, 25–27, 29–35, 41, 44–46, 53, 56–57, 60–63, 65, 66, 67, 68–69, 71–73, 77–78
philosophy
  of disability, 3–4, 5–6, 11, 12, 51–53, 73–74, 76, 77, 78–79
  feminist, 8, 72, 98n.34
  lyric, 54
  moral, 2–3, 36–37, 52, 67–69, 70–74, 79–80
  of music, 3, 8, 12, 15, 25, 77–79
presence, 12, 17, 21, 27–28, 38, 45–46, 56, 61, 69–70, 71–72, 73–74, 81

race, racism, ix, 8, 44–45, 48–49, 52, 78, 88n.8, 98n.34
recognition, 11, 37, 39–40, 44, 46–47, 48, 53, 60, 61, 69, 71, 75–76
Rousseau, Jean-Jacques, 38, 39–40, 45–46

Sacks, Oliver, 27–28, 33, 105n.53
sameness, 11, 37–46, 48, 49, 58, 60
savants, 8–9, 33, 45–47
Schutz, Alfred, 12, 17, 22, 60–62
security
  existential, 10–11, 19, 23–24, 62
  ontological, 54–55, 64
  philosophical, 54
self, 5–6, 10–11, 59, 77. *See also* communication
  musical, 19–35
  as performative, 8, 10–11, 26, 33–34, 75
self-expression, 10–11, 25–26, 29, 33–34, 35, 40–41, 49–50, 62–63, 67
silence, 48, 54–55, 56–57, 81–82
solidarity, 12, 31, 70–71, 74
sonification, 2, 4–5, 11, 13, 77, 81–82
  definition, 4
  of difference, 11, 46–51 (*see* difference)
  philosophical, 5, 52–53, 77
  of sameness, 11, 37–46 (*see* sameness)
  of self, 19–35, 40, 41–43, 80
spaces, 20–21, 22–23, 31, 34, 35, 56, 57, 58
  cultural, 79–80
  institutional, x, 20, 28, 63
  musical, 12, 34–35, 61, 62, 63–64, 66, 69, 75–76, 79–80
  performance, 29–30, 50–51, 63
Straus, Joseph, 16–17, 29–30, 32–33, 46–48, 49–50, 78–79
suffering, 10–11, 26–27, 28–29, 48, 49, 78
Swinburne, Jan, 81–82

temporality
  music as temporal art, 15–16, 21–24, 54–55, 57, 62
  and self, 23–25, 34
time, 15, 48, 81–82. *See* temporality
  musical, 12, 21–23, 34, 57, 62–63, 65, 66, 69, 81–82
Tsujii, Nobu, 1–2, 77–78

virtues, 12, 70–74, 77
Vorhaus, John, 33–34, 42–43, 67, 80
vulnerability, x, 24, 55, 70–71, 72–73, 74

Warren, Jeff, 23, 60, 63, 74
West, Cornel, 28, 48, 49
Williams syndrome, 33
Wittgenstein, Ludwig, 58
wordlessness, 11, 55–57, 59
worldlessness, 11, 57, 59

worlds, 57, 81
   musical, 12, 13, 21, 26, 34, 35, 38–39, 54–55, 57, 64, 67, 68–69, 76, 77–80
   philosophical, 2–3
   sonic, 11

Zwicky, Jan, 54–56, 60